Job Hunting
for ROOKIES

Titles in the *for* ROOKIES series

About the author

Dr Rob Yeung is widely regarded as a top business speaker and authority on the psychology of high achievement. A director at leadership consulting firm Talentspace, he spends most of his time coaching leaders and their teams to accomplish their goals. He frequently interviews candidates on behalf of employers, and has become an expert on what it takes to get fulfilling, high-earning jobs.

He appears frequently on television as an expert, spanning programmes such as CNN and ITN News to *Big Brother* and the BBC's *Working Lunch*. He presents the BBC TV series *How to Get Your Dream Job*. He has written over a dozen best-selling books and is frequently quoted in the press, including the *Financial Times* and *Guardian* newspapers.

Job Hunting
for ROOKIES

First published in 2009 by

Marshall Cavendish Limited
Fifth Floor
32–38 Saffron Hill
London EC1N 8FH
United Kingdom
T: +44 (0)20 7421 8120
F: +44 (0)20 7421 8121
sales@marshallcavendish.co.uk
www.marshallcavendish.co.uk

A member of **BPR**

businesspublishersroundtable.com

Marshall Cavendish is a trademark of Times Publishing Limited

Other Marshall Cavendish offices: Marshall Cavendish International (Asia) Private
Limited, 1 New Industrial Road, Singapore 536196 • Marshall Cavendish Corporation.
99 White Plains Road, Tarrytown NY 10591–9001, USA • Marshall Cavendish International
(Thailand) Co Ltd. 253 Asoke, 12th Floor, Sukhumvit 21 Road, Klongtoey Nua, Wattana,
Bangkok 10110, Thailand • Marshall Cavendish (Malaysia) Sdn Bhd, Times Subang, Lot 46,
Subang Hi-Tech Industrial Park, Batu Tiga, 40000 Shah Alam, Selangor Darul Ehsan,
Malaysia

A CIP record for this book is available from the British Library

ISBN 978-0-462-09956-9

Illustrations by Nuria Aparicio and Joan Guardiet

Printed and bound in Great Britain by
TJ International Limited, Padstow, Cornwall

Contents

- If you need help negotiating a good deal before you sign on the dotted line, head for Chapter 10 too.

If any of those situations is affecting you, then look no further. This book can help. It's up to you how you use this book – just make sure you do use it! It can't help you to get a job if it merely sits on the side of your desk or on a shelf!

Get ready to succeed

You *can* get the job you want. A lot of candidates fail because they don't understand the rules of getting a new job. They make basic mistakes in pulling together their applications or foul up during the interview process. However, you will not fall into the traps that befall other candidates.

So long as you apply the advice in this book, you will gain yourself an enormous advantage over other candidates. With diligence and effort on your part, you will succeed. Ready to get started? Let's go!

Let's start with a bit of diagnosis. Before you run off looking for a new job, let's look at your skills, qualities, and interests. What sort of job *should* you be looking for?

CHAPTER 1

Setting your sights on what you want

Finding the work you want

The first step in finding a new job is deciding what kind of work you want to do. Now, you may be thinking, I know exactly what I want to do. But let me ask you this: are you 100 per cent happy in your current work? Whether you are currently in work or out of work, does the prospect of your job have you jumping out of bed in the mornings, excited at the mere thought of it?

If you love or at least like the work you do, you will find it much easier to get a job. There is so much competition for jobs these days that if you see your work as a chore, you will not be able to convince an interviewer to hire you. Why should they give you the job when they can hire someone else who is genuinely enthusiastic about it?

So before you throw yourself into the hard work of looking for a job, spend at least a little time thinking about what your new job should be. Let's work through a handful of exercises to uncover what you could be doing next.

12

Rookie Buster

If you love or at least like the work you do, you will find it much easier to get a job.

Understanding the product that is you

When people are happy in their work, they usually work harder and end up being more successful too. And people are happy and successful when they get to combine their skills, personal traits and interests in their work.

Let's get started with three exercises that will help you to learn more about yourself.

Self-Discovery 1: Understanding your skills

If you are good with people, you will thrive in an environment in which you can work with colleagues and customers. If you have a knack for technology, you may need to look for work with computers and gadgets. Or if you can handle numbers easily, then working with budgets or in finance may be where you should go. The more you get to use your talents on a daily basis at work, the more contented and productive you will be.

Look at the following list of skill-verbs. Put one tick next to each verb that you believe you possess. And put another tick next to it if you enjoy applying that skill. For example, I know that I'm actually quite good at numbers, so I'd put one tick next to "calculating". But I don't really enjoy having to pore over numbers, so I would not add a second tick next to it. Whereas I am good at coaching people and I enjoy it too – so "coaching" would get two ticks.

Rookie Buster

The more you get to use your talents on a daily basis at work, the more contented and productive you will be.

Acting	☐	☐	Detecting	☐	☐	Initiating	☐	☐
Adapting	☐	☐	Determining	☐	☐	Innovating	☐	☐
Addressing	☐	☐	Developing	☐	☐	Inspecting	☐	☐
Administering	☐	☐	Devising	☐	☐	Inspiring	☐	☐
Advising	☐	☐	Diagnosing	☐	☐	Installing	☐	☐
Analysing	☐	☐	Directing	☐	☐	Instructing	☐	☐
Answering	☐	☐	Discovering	☐	☐	Interpreting	☐	☐
Anticipating	☐	☐	Dispensing	☐	☐	Interviewing	☐	☐
Arbitrating	☐	☐	Displaying	☐	☐	Inventing	☐	☐
Arranging	☐	☐	Disproving	☐	☐	Inventorying	☐	☐
Assembling	☐	☐	Distributing	☐	☐	Investigating	☐	☐
Assessing	☐	☐	Drawing	☐	☐	Judging	☐	☐
Auditing	☐	☐	Driving	☐	☐	Keeping	☐	☐
Budgeting	☐	☐	Editing	☐	☐	Leading	☐	☐
Building	☐	☐	Eliminating	☐	☐	Learning	☐	☐
Calculating	☐	☐	Empathizing	☐	☐	Lecturing	☐	☐
Calling	☐	☐	Enforcing	☐	☐	Listening	☐	☐
Charting	☐	☐	Estimating	☐	☐	Maintaining	☐	☐
Checking	☐	☐	Evaluating	☐	☐	Making	☐	☐
Classifying	☐	☐	Examining	☐	☐	Managing	☐	☐
Coaching	☐	☐	Experimenting	☐	☐	Manipulating	☐	☐
Collecting	☐	☐	Explaining	☐	☐	Mediating	☐	☐
Communicating	☐	☐	Extracting	☐	☐	Meeting	☐	☐
Compiling	☐	☐	Fixing	☐	☐	Mentoring	☐	☐
Completing	☐	☐	Formulating	☐	☐	Modelling	☐	☐
Composing	☐	☐	Gathering	☐	☐	Monitoring	☐	☐
Computing	☐	☐	Generating	☐	☐	Motivating	☐	☐
Conducting	☐	☐	Giving	☐	☐	Negotiating	☐	☐
Conserving	☐	☐	Guiding	☐	☐	Observing	☐	☐
Consolidating	☐	☐	Handling	☐	☐	Operating	☐	☐
Constructing	☐	☐	Helping	☐	☐	Ordering	☐	☐
Controlling	☐	☐	Hypothesizing	☐	☐	Organizing	☐	☐
Coordinating	☐	☐	Identifying	☐	☐	Overseeing	☐	☐
Coping	☐	☐	Illustrating	☐	☐	Painting	☐	☐
Counselling	☐	☐	Imagining	☐	☐	Performing	☐	☐
Creating	☐	☐	Improving	☐	☐	Persuading	☐	☐
Deciding	☐	☐	Improvising	☐	☐	Photographing	☐	☐
Defining	☐	☐	Increasing	☐	☐	Planning	☐	☐
Delivering	☐	☐	Influencing	☐	☐	Predicting	☐	☐
Designing	☐	☐	Informing	☐	☐	Preparing	☐	☐

14

Prescribing	☐	☐	Reporting	☐	☐	Supplying	☐	☐
Presenting	☐	☐	Representing	☐	☐	Synthesizing	☐	☐
Problem solving	☐	☐	Researching	☐	☐	Talking	☐	☐
Processing	☐	☐	Resolving	☐	☐	Teaching	☐	☐
Producing	☐	☐	Responding	☐	☐	Team-building	☐	☐
Programming	☐	☐	Restoring	☐	☐	Telling	☐	☐
Promoting	☐	☐	Retrieving	☐	☐	Tending	☐	☐
Proofreading	☐	☐	Reviewing	☐	☐	Testing	☐	☐
Protecting	☐	☐	Risking	☐	☐	Training	☐	☐
Providing	☐	☐	Scheduling	☐	☐	Transcribing	☐	☐
Purchasing	☐	☐	Selecting	☐	☐	Translating	☐	☐
Questioning	☐	☐	Selling	☐	☐	Travelling	☐	☐
Reading	☐	☐	Serving	☐	☐	Treating	☐	☐
Recommending	☐	☐	Setting	☐	☐	Trouble-shooting	☐	☐
Reconciling	☐	☐	Shaping	☐	☐	Tutoring	☐	☐
Recording	☐	☐	Sharing	☐	☐	Typing	☐	☐
Recruiting	☐	☐	Showing	☐	☐	Understanding	☐	☐
Reducing	☐	☐	Sketching	☐	☐	Uniting	☐	☐
Referring	☐	☐	Solving	☐	☐	Upgrading	☐	☐
Rehabilitating	☐	☐	Sorting	☐	☐	Using	☐	☐
Relating	☐	☐	Speaking	☐	☐	Utilizing	☐	☐
Remembering	☐	☐	Studying	☐	☐	Working	☐	☐
Rendering	☐	☐	Summarizing	☐	☐	Writing	☐	☐
Repairing	☐	☐	Supervising	☐	☐			

When you've assigned your ticks, take a look at your list. For each skill-verb that you put two ticks against, have a think what that skill could relate to. For example, if you enjoy communicating, *what* do you communicate? *What* do you test? *What* do you repair?

When you're ready, let's move on to the next exercise.

Self-Discovery 2: Highlighting your characteristics and qualities

Your skills are an important part of who you are. But you also probably have certain characteristics and qualities that influence how you deal with the world too.

If you are naturally someone who pays attention to detail, you will do well in a job that allows you to be careful and precise. But if you hate attention to detail, make sure you find a job that allows you to steer clear of the small stuff. If you are collaborative, you should probably look for a job that allows you to work with a team rather than one that insists you work mainly on your own.

Put a tick against any of the following words that describe you. If you're not sure, why not ask a couple of friends how they would describe you too?

Accountable	☐	Efficient	☐	Passionate	☐
Accurate	☐	Emotional	☐	Patient	☐
Adaptable	☐	Encouraging	☐	Persistent	☐
Aggressive	☐	Energetic	☐	Persuasive	☐
Ambitious	☐	Ethical	☐	Practical	☐
Analytical	☐	Flexible	☐	Polite	☐
Articulate	☐	Forgiving	☐	Quick	☐
Calm	☐	Friendly	☐	Quiet	☐
Careful	☐	Fun-loving	☐	Reliable	☐
Collaborative	☐	Generous	☐	Resilient	☐
Compassionate	☐	Helpful	☐	Resourceful	☐
Competitive	☐	Honest	☐	Sensitive	☐
Composed	☐	Imaginative	☐	Spontaneous	☐
Confident	☐	Influential	☐	Stable	☐
Conscientious	☐	Innovative	☐	Strategic	☐
Consistent	☐	Inquisitive	☐	Supportive	☐
Courageous	☐	Inspirational	☐	Sympathetic	☐
Creative	☐	Logical	☐	Tactful	☐
Critical	☐	Loyal	☐	Thorough	☐
Daring	☐	Mature	☐	Thoughtful	☐
Dedicated	☐	Methodical	☐	Tough	☐
Detail-oriented	☐	Meticulous	☐	Trustworthy	☐
Direct	☐	Neat	☐	Upbeat	☐
Discreet	☐	Numerate	☐	Understanding	☐
Driven	☐	Observant	☐	Visionary	☐
Dutiful	☐	Open-minded	☐		
Dynamic	☐	Organized	☐		

Now, you may feel that quite a lot of those words could describe you. But if you could only choose ten of them to describe you, which ten would you choose? Write them down on a separate sheet of paper.

Self-Discovery 3: Identifying your interests

Next, let's think about the topics or subjects that most interest you. Ask yourself the following questions:

- If you could talk about any topic, what would that subject or field of

16   interest be? For example, it could be antiques, the environment, food and cookery, mechanics or engineering, schools, overseas travel, religion, technology, photography, animals – and so on.

- What topics do you find yourself drawn to when you pick up a newspaper or magazine – such as finance, fashion, politics, home interiors, science, education, health and exercise, art, business, etc?
- What kinds of roles and job sectors appeal to you? For example, advertising, law, car industry, banking, manufacturing, pharmaceuticals, administration, public sector, textiles, and so on.

Narrowing your focus

Now look back at your skills, your characteristics and qualities, and your interests. Do any jobs pop into your head? Do you get a flash of inspiration, an "a-ha!" moment, telling you what you should be pursuing for your next job?

Don't worry if you don't have a clear idea yet. I'm going to guide you step-to-step to finding the right kind of work for you. First of all, you need to summarize the product that is you:

1. Go back to the exercise on strengths and pull out your top three to five skills. This handful of skills should be the ones that stand out as being of the most importance to you. Get a fresh sheet of paper and write down the heading "Skills", then write down these three to five skills beneath it.
2. Go back to the exercise on qualities and characteristics and transfer the top five of those to this new sheet of paper under the heading "Qualities and Characteristics".
3. Next, look back at the exercise on interests and identify your top three to five areas of interests – write these down under "Interests".

Next, you are going to tap into your greatest resource: other people. If you are to find your way to the right job for you, you must talk to people and seek their advice:

1. Show your summary sheet of paper to at least half-a-dozen

friends. Buy them a drink; take them out for a coffee. Pick up the telephone or drop them an email if you can't get to speak to them. Explain that you'd like to find a job that allows you to apply your strengths, characteristics and qualities, and interests too. Ask them for their thoughts. Let them think and see what they can come up with.

2. Let your friends talk, and scribble down everything that they suggest. Their ideas may not make sense initially – they may seem irrelevant or frankly silly. But wait until you have spoken to the half-dozen people before you look back at the notes you have made. If they recommend that you speak to other people, go and do it. If they suggest that you should do some book research or check something out on the internet, do that too. But remember that people – not books or the internet – are your biggest resource. Even if you would much rather depend on your own reading, thinking, and resourcefulness, I can guarantee you that other people (and not you yourself) will help you to find inspiration.

3. If you don't come up with any ideas from your first half-dozen friends, reach out to another half-dozen people. And keep repeating this until you hit that brainwave.

Keep an open mind. You may not find a job that exactly matches every single one of your talents and interests. But by talking to other people, you may surprise yourself by finding a job that matches *many* of them. When you find the right job, you should feel excited – you will *know* that you're on track to finding a great new career for you.

18

Rookie Buster

When you find the right job, you should feel excited – you will *know* that you're on track to finding a great new career for you.

Checking that it's the right choice for you

If you're not sure about the types of jobs that you or your friends come up with, you need to do a bit more digging.

Go to visit places where those jobs are and talk to the people doing those jobs. If you think you'd like to work for an airline, go and visit the airport and soak up the atmosphere. If you think you'd like to work with landscape gardeners, visit a garden centre and chat to the staff. You will almost always find that people are happy to talk about their jobs.

If it's impractical for you to turn up at their place of work, get in touch with the trade body or association that looks after people who do that line of work. For example, if you think you may want to train as a veterinary nurse, type "veterinary nurse association" into your favourite internet search engine and give the association a call.

In talking to the various people you meet, you may want to ask questions such as:

- "How did you get into this type of work?"
- "How do you spend your time on a daily basis?"
- "What do you most enjoy about it?"
- "What frustrates you about it?"
- "What sort of training did you need to do to get into this career?"

By talking to enough people, you should be able to decide whether a   19
particular type of job or field of interest really is sufficiently exciting
for you to pursue.

Setting goals for an effective job hunt

When you have decided on the kind of work you want to pursue, you
can get started on finding it.

Writing your mission statement

To help you retain your focus for an effective job hunt, you should
write a mission statement that summarizes what you are looking for.
This statement will act as a reminder not only of what you are looking
for, but also of what you can bring to an employer.

Here's an example of a completed mission statement and how it's
broken down [shown in brackets]:

> I am looking for a job as a <u>branch banking manager</u> [job title],
> which will allow me to apply my key skills in <u>leading a team of
> people, analysing numbers, advising customers and persuading
> them to use the bank's services</u> [skills from Self-Discovery 1]. I
> believe that I am a <u>calm, competitive, confident, honest</u>
> [characteristics and qualities from Self-Discovery 2] person –
> and I will use those qualities to do my best in my work. If at all
> possible, I will seek to combine my work with my interests in
> <u>cars, computers and the health industries</u> [interests from Self-
> Discovery 3].

20   Now it's your turn. Fill in the blanks by looking back at the results of
your three Self-Discovery exercises:

> I am looking for a job as a _____[job title],
> which will allow me to apply my key skills in [skills from Self-
> Discovery 1] _____
> _____. I believe that I am a
> [characteristics and qualities from Self-Discovery 2] _____
> _____ person – and I will
> use those qualities to do my best in my work. If at all possible, I
> will seek to combine my work with my interests in [interests
> from Self-Discovery 3]_____
>
> _____.

When you have completed your mission statement, you can use it to
keep you on course as you go about your job hunting activities.

Putting in the work

Now you can get started in looking for a job. However, the first thing
you need to realize is that it's called "job hunting" for a reason. Jobs
won't just land in your lap. Employers will not seek you out to offer you
a job.

It is up to *you* to track down suitable employers. It is up to *you* to
convince them that they should give you a shot. *You* need to put in the
hard work, the hours, and the effort. Your likelihood of finding a great
new job is in direct proportion to the quality and quantity of effort you
put into your job hunting.

Rookie Buster

Your likelihood of finding a great new job is in direct proportion to the quality and quantity of effort you put into your job hunting.

Assuming you're doing the right stuff and spending your time productively, if you spend ten hours a week on your job hunt, you will probably find a job twice as quickly as someone who is spending only five hours a week on it. Now that may sound totally obvious – but it does need saying for some people (and I apologize if you are not one of them).

Quite often I come across people who complain that they can't find a new job. But when I ask them what they are doing, they say that they spend just a couple of hours a week clicking on job websites, picking up the occasional newspaper, and sending off an application or two.

To get a new job, you need to view job hunting as your new job. If you are unemployed, you need to think of your job hunt as your new full-time occupation. You should get up and be ready for eight or ten hours' work every day. If you're currently employed, look at your job hunt as an additional, part-time job that you will have to squeeze in alongside your normal weekly activities in order to find a better job.

Rookie Buster

To get a new job, you need to view job hunting as your new job.

But the good news is that you *can* get a new job. Work diligently at it and you *will* get a new, better job.

Coach's notes

- Remember that people who can apply their talents on a daily basis are both more satisfied and more successful in their work than people who can't.
- Think about how you and other people would describe you. Understanding your personality traits and the qualities that make you who you are will help you to find work that allows you to be yourself at work.
- Wouldn't you rather work in a field that interests you than one that feels like a constant chore? Figure out the topics and job sectors that appeal to you, and you can focus your job hunting efforts accordingly.
- Understand that other people are a huge resource. Talk to other people to help you generate ideas for jobs that you could do.
- Write up your mission statement to help you keep focused in your job hunt.
- Realize that it's up to you to put in the hours and effort to land a new job – it isn't going to happen on its own!

Go for it! Do take the time to figure out what kind of work you should be looking for. Too many people start their job-seeking campaigns by immediately looking for more of what they've always done. But if you aren't excited by the idea of your work, how can you expect to be enthusiastic in chasing up job leads? If you're passionate about what you want, you're already halfway to convincing an employer to hire you!

24 **Notes**

Notes

Employers are usually inundated with many applications for every job they advertise. But you will get yourself noticed. In this chapter, I share with you exactly what it is that employers are looking for, so you can tell them exactly why you're perfect for the job.

CHAPTER 2

Understanding what employers want

Appreciating the skills and qualities that employers want

Most employers believe that certain skills and qualities are essential in the people that they hire. And if you can show an employer that you have those skills and qualities, you can help yourself to stand out from the rest of the crowd.

Surveys frequently ask employers what they want from the people they hire, and I am going to share with you the top skills that employers talk about again and again. Employers may not always mention all of these top skills and qualities in the job advertisements that they place. Sometimes they just assume that candidates will have them.

Bear in mind that different employers emphasize certain skills and qualities over others – it's up to you to figure out what's important and what's not. Suppose an organization is looking to fill a job for a sales person who will travel up and down the country to visit customers. As the sales person would be spending a lot more time with customers than colleagues, the organization would probably look for candidates who have influence and persuasion skills (in other words selling skills) more than team working skills.

28 Have a look through the following skills and qualities, and bear them constantly in mind as you start your job hunt.

Rookie Buster

Bear in mind that different employers emphasize certain skills and qualities over others – it's up to you to figure out what's important and what's not.

Communication skills

Employers want to hire people who can communicate thoughts and ideas with other people. Of course, there are different ways to communicate, so consider:

- Communicating face-to-face with other people by talking, listening, and sharing ideas.
- Having a good telephone manner – being able to speak and be understood clearly.
- Communicating in writing, for example in letters, emails, and other documents.

Influence and persuasion

Employers don't just want people who can communicate by telling others what they should be doing. No one likes to be told what to do all of the time. So employers prize influence and persuasion skills too. Employers look for people who can win others over or change their minds. Examples of influence and persuasion include:

- Getting other people to change their point of view.
- Convincing others to pursue a course of action or recommendation of yours.
- Talking customers or clients into buying products or services.

Team work 29

I'm sure you hear about this one all the time. Most employers want to hire people who will help each other out rather than focus only on what each individual is supposed to be doing. Elements of good team working include:

- Helping colleagues or other members of the team with practical problems such as too much workload.
- Giving advice to other people at work to help them do their jobs – even when helping them isn't necessarily part of your job.
- Keeping the morale of the team up by being positive and enthusiastic.

Problem solving

Employers want to hire people who can take on difficulties or challenges and work out how to deal with them. For example, this could include:

- Looking at a problem and coming up with different ideas or options for handling it.
- Breaking complex problems down into smaller issues that are more easily handled.
- Weighing up the pros and cons of different options or choices and finally taking a course of action to handle the situation.

Planning and organizing

I'm sure you won't be surprised to hear that organizational skills are in high demand. Employers look out for people who can make plans and organize their workload. This might include:

- Organizing your own workload – for example, when you have too much work to do, being able to

30 prioritize what's important and what's less important, in order to ensure you get important work completed.
- Managing projects by making plans to ensure that everything gets done and nothing gets forgotten.
- Coordinating with other people to get large pieces of work done; and delivering them on time and on budget.

Adaptability and flexibility

Employers don't want to hire people who will work in a rigid or inflexible manner. They want to hire people who can be accommodating and willing to change their plans or their minds if necessary. Being adaptable and flexible includes behaviour such as:
- Being willing to stay late or come into work early occasionally to help the rest of the team out when there's a lot of work on (and being punctual all of the rest of the time).
- Offering to help other people with their workload even though their work may not strictly be part of your job description.
- Being willing to listen to other people's opinions and staying open-minded enough to change your mind when they have a valid argument.

Drive and initiative

You may have heard employers sometimes talk about wanting to hire people who are "self-starters". They want people who are self-motivated and willing to put more effort in when the work gets tough. This may include:
- Being able to handle setbacks by trying harder.
- Looking for different approaches rather than giving up in the face of adversity.
- Being on the lookout for newer and better ways of doing things rather than simply accepting inefficiencies and problems at work.

The human touch   31

Now, employers probably won't ever use the phrase "the human touch". But I use the phrase to mean a bunch of qualities that includes warmth, humour and integrity. After all, who wants to work with an efficient but cold and emotionless robot? Consider:

- Being upbeat and enthusiastic.
- Having a positive attitude.
- Being friendly and approachable to colleagues, customers, and anyone else you may need to deal with.

Understanding organizational goals

Demonstrating that you have the necessary skills and qualities will help you in the right direction towards getting a new job – but that gets you only part of the way. To secure a job, you need to demonstrate that you can use your skills and qualities to help employers to achieve their goals. Most organizations have goals that are some combination of the following:

- Making money.
- Reducing costs/saving money.
- Getting things done more quickly.
- Making work easier.
- Growing the size of the organization.
- Developing people within the organization, for example by coaching and mentoring them.
- Attracting new customers or clients.
- Retaining customers or clients.
- Promoting a message or the brand and image of the organization to people outside the organization.

Not all organizations have the same goals. For example, an investment bank may be highly motivated by making money, while a children's charity may be more interested in promoting its particular message. But if you can figure out the goals that interest different employers, you

32 can very quickly learn how to make yourself a lot more attractive to them as an applicant.

Rookie Buster

To secure a job, you need to demonstrate that you can use your skills and qualities to help employers to achieve their goals.

Deciphering job adverts

The job advert is an important source of information in your hunt for a job. It tells you what you should emphasize or leave off your CV. And, once you get invited along to an interview, it tells you about likely questions that you may be asked.

In putting together your application for a job, have a thorough read of the employer's job advert. A good tip: use a highlighter pen to pick out key words and phrases that alert you to the kinds of skills, qualities and goals achieved that an employer is looking for in the ideal candidate.

Rookie Buster

Use a highlighter pen to pick out key words and phrases that alert you to the kinds of skills, qualities and goals achieved that an employer is looking for in the ideal candidate.

Job advert: example 1

Have a look at the following job advert:

> **LAW FIRM SEEKS PERSONAL ASSISTANT TO CHAIRMAN**
> Jackson, Kennedy & Anderson Partners (JKA) is looking for a personal assistant to support the Chairman of the firm. The successful candidate must:
> - Have excellent communication skills – you will deal with senior clients both over the telephone and when they visit the office too.
> - Possess good computer skills – you must be able to use word processing, email, and diary management packages to assist the Chairman with all of his secretarial needs.
> - Be capable of working to tight deadlines to meet the needs of both the Chairman and external clients.
>
> £ dependent on experience.
> Email: anna.peterson@jka-partners.com

So what key words and phrases catch your attention? What skills and qualities do you think you would need to include on your CV? What skills and qualities do you think you would need to speak about if you were invited along to an interview?

Looking at the advert, we can deduce that:

- As the job is looking for a "personal assistant", you will stand the best chance of getting the job if you have already been a personal assistant in the past. You'd have an even better chance of getting the job if you have previously worked under a senior person such as the chairman of a firm, the managing director, or at least another high-ranking manager.
- "Excellent communication skills" are a must-have. I would recommend that you take that phrase and repeat it in a prominent place on your CV to catch the employer's attention. And, if you

34 were to go along to an interview, of course you would have to explain exactly why you believe you have "excellent communication skills".

- "Good computer skills" similarly dictates that you should repeat that phrase on your CV. If you have experience of particular programs or software packages, you may need to list them on your CV and/or be ready to talk about them during an interview.
- The phrase "working to tight deadlines" also looks important. Again, a good tactic when putting together a CV is to repeat back key phrases that the employer has mentioned. Plus, if you get invited to an interview, you would need to give examples of times when you have worked to tight deadlines too.

Job advert: example 2

Here's a different job advert:

> **GROWING COMPANY SEEKS COMPUTER SALES EXECUTIVE**
> Opportunity to join growing IT company for two sales executives with experience of selling both hardware and software. You would ideally have knowledge of the Zeta2 and ORKM hardware systems. You must have exceptional relationship building skills and a proven track record of selling to owner-managers and IT managers in small- and medium-sized organizations. You must enjoy travelling extensively. Call Peter Maxwell on 01307 991 6701 for further details and an application form.

Certain key phrases suggest how you should go about trying to get this job:

- The advert mentions sales and selling three times ("sales executives", "selling", and "a proven track record of selling"). Given that this employer is so interested in sales and selling, you should

probably describe in quite a lot of detail on your CV the sales
experience that you have. At interview, you would also have to be
ready to talk at length about your sales experience.

- "Selling both hardware and software" implies that you must
mention your experience of selling both hardware and software.
- "Knowledge of the Zeta2 and ORKM hardware systems" suggests
that your application would be much
stronger if you mention these two
systems on your CV. However, the fact
that the advert says that you should
"ideally" have them means that you
may still have a shot at the job even if
you do not have direct experience of
them. But do mention any related
systems that you are familiar with.
- "Exceptional relationship building
skills" suggests that you should use this
phrase on your CV too. In order to get an
employer's attention, there's nothing like
repeating back to an employer exactly how you
match up to what they are looking for.
- Another key phrase is: "Selling to owner-managers and IT
managers in small- and medium-sized organizations." If you can
genuinely mention how you have sold to owner-managers and IT
managers in the past, particular in small- and medium-sized
businesses, you will almost certainly become a very attractive
candidate.
- The phrase "enjoy travelling extensively" indicates that you should
mention this both on your CV and during interview too.

Researching employers

Employers like to feel special. They don't just want to hire people who
have the skills and qualities that will help them to achieve their goals.
Employers want to hire people who *want* to work for their particular

36 organization over any others. And in order to demonstrate that you want to work for any particular employer, you have to do some research.

Rookie Buster

Employers want to hire people who *want* to work for their particular organization over any others.

At a minimum, you should be able to answer the following questions about the employer:

- **What sort of work does the organization do?** What services or products does the organization offer?
- **Who are the key people within the organization?** If you can find out the names of the founders, the managing director, any of the board members, or other senior people, you can look them up online and find out about their backgrounds.
- **Who are the organization's competitors?** What products and services do those competitors provide?
- **How is this organization special?** Many employers are actually very similar to their competitors. However, almost all organizations at least *believe* themselves to be special and different from their competitors. In what ways?
- **What is going on with the organization?** What events are affecting the organization either right now or in the future? What are the trends and issues facing the organization and the general sector?

Going online

Thankfully, the internet has made researching employers a lot easier. Here are some great sources of information about the organization and its work:

- **Their own website**. Nowadays, even fairly small organizations often have their own websites. Telephone the company and ask for its web address – you may find useful information such as their annual report, press releases, news and basic facts about what the organization does, its aims and ambitions.
- **Your favourite search engine**. I use Google, but you may prefer some other search engine. Tap the name of the company into a search engine and you will probably find all sorts of news and snippets about the organization. Also type the name of the industry (for example, publishing, education, financial services, the non-profit sector) or the job title of the profession (such as social worker, chemical engineer, human resources officer) into the search engine too. That way you will gain a solid appreciation of both the job you are applying for and the sector or industry in which the organization operates.

Getting up close and personal

Going online and reading up on an employer is a good start. But you can get a lot more information by getting out and about too. Make sure you:

- **Visit any physical locations and premises**. Make sure you go along to any shops, branches, salons, showrooms, etc. And to get an appreciation of what the organization's competitors do, make sure you visit them too. Try to buy, use, or otherwise get a feel for the organization's services or products.
- **Talk to people who are associated with the organization**. Pop into any shops, branches or showrooms, and talk to the staff. Tell them that you are considering working for the organization and ask them for their thoughts. You may even get advice on how to put together a better application!

Rookie Buster

Try to buy, use, or otherwise get a feel for the organization's services or products.

Coach's notes

For each organization you want to apply to, you must:

- Work out the list of skills and qualities that the employer is looking for. Bear in mind that the employer may mention some of these in the job advert. However, others may be implied. It's up to you to figure out what to put on your CV to grab the employer's attention.
- Consider the organization's goals. Once you have worked out what the organization is trying to achieve, you can put together examples of how you have delivered similar outcomes for previous employers.
- Keep a copy of every job advert that you apply for. This is the single richest source of information that will tell you both what to put on your CV and what to talk about at interview.
- Remember that employers like to feel special – and you can make them feel special by demonstrating the amount of information and insights you have dug up about them.
- Do go online for research – but don't rely on it. Visiting premises and talking to staff can give you access to information about the organization and what's happening to it that isn't available on the internet.

Go for it! Make sure you do some research! Yes, yes, I know it takes time. But it's time well spent. Think of research as a weapon to keep you ahead of the competition. Do just a couple of hours of research for each job that you apply for and you give yourself the very best chance of getting the job. You can do it!

40 **Notes**

Notes

Your CV is usually your first point of contact with an organization. Long before employers have the chance to meet you in person, they need to be impressed by the document that is your CV. In this chapter, I tell you how to grab an employer's attention, how to steer clear of common traps and pitfalls, and why you need to have *many* CVs rather than just the one.

CHAPTER 3

Constructing a solid CV

Tailoring individual CVs

Most job adverts receive many dozens – if not hundreds – of applications. In order to decide whom to invite to interview, the employer may spend as little as a minute glancing through each CV.

So savvy job seekers do everything in their power to help the employer to see immediately how they stack up to the requirements of the job. And they do this by tailoring each and every CV they send out.

Gone are the days of creating a single CV and sending it to every organization you might want to work for. Sure, that used to be standard practice maybe 10 or 15 years ago. But the job market is much more competitive now. And to keep up, you need to tailor every single CV you send out. Even if you are sending out CVs for the same type of job to companies that you think are very similar, you will get the best results by tailoring each CV. If you don't, you will almost certainly end up on the employer's discard pile.

Rookie Buster

Gone are the days of creating a single CV and sending it to every organization you might want to work for.

Why tailor?

Let's work through an example and you'll see why tailoring your CV is so very important. Suppose you are applying for a job as an office administrator and are faced with the two following job adverts:

ABC Banking Corporation	**XYZ Home Trading**
Business administrator needed to track loan applications from inception through to rejection or acceptance; produce monthly status reports for senior management; and file additional documentation and maintain database.	Administrative officer needed to join head office team of this growing retailer. Role involves using spreadsheets and databases to keep track of inventory movements from suppliers through warehousing and to stores.
Qualities required:	The successful candidate must have strong administration skills and communication skills with both junior and senior people. Experience within a customer-facing environment is required. Excellent attention to detail and ability to work to tight deadlines desirable.
• Excellent administrative skills • Creativity and willingness to use initiative • Ability to multi-task • Excellent written and verbal communication skills • Exceptional organization skills	

Most job hunters include a section on their CVs using the heading of "Key Skills". So what key skills would you highlight in applying for these two jobs?

As you can see, ABC Banking Corporation asks for someone with "excellent administrative skills" while XYZ Home Trading is looking for someone with "strong administration skills". Those two phrases are very similar so you could use either phrase interchangeably on both the CV you send to ABC as well as XYZ.

ABC then lists "creativity and willingness to use initiative", "ability to multi-task", "excellent written and verbal communication skills", and "exceptional organization skills". The job at XYZ may in fact be very similar to the job at ABC, but XYZ has emphasized that it is looking for "communication skills with both junior and senior people", "experience within a customer-facing environment", "excellent attention to detail" and "ability to work to tight deadlines."

So while it would be a good idea to list "creativity and willingness to use initiative" in the CV you send to ABC, you would gain no points for listing it in the CV you send to XYZ. And while XYZ clearly wants to hire someone with "experience within a cus-tomer-facing environment", why should ABC be at all interested if you mention that fact on your CV to them?

Make a clear connection

Now, you may think that both employers should be able to read between the lines, make the connection and tell that you are a good administrator. But remember that the employer is inundated with many, many CVs! The employer is probably tired of reading through CVs. The employer's attention may wander. So you need to make the link between your skills and what the organization is looking for. You need to make the link blindingly obvious.

If an employer is looking for certain skills or qualities, you use their precise wording on your CV. If they say "leadership skills", you say "leadership skills", not "management skills". If they say "managing risk", you don't say "avoiding risk" or "being cautious", you say "manag-ing risk". Nothing beats repeating back to employers the precise, exact profile of the person they are looking for.

Rookie Buster

If an employer is looking for certain skills or qualities, you use their precise wording on your CV.

Matching what you have with what the employer wants

Skills and knowledge

To begin tailoring your CV, take a sheet of paper and draw a line down the middle, from top to bottom. Now take a look at the job advert and list on the left-hand side of the page all of the skills and knowledge the employer is looking for.

Once you've done that, list on the right-hand side of the page all of the skills and knowledge that you have that could be relevant. Bear in mind that some of the skills and knowledge you possess may have been gained in either paid employment or unpaid work such as volunteering, your studies, or bringing up a family.

Qualifications and training

Get a clean sheet of paper and again draw a line down the middle from top to bottom. Write down the different qualifications and training that the employer needs on the left side of the sheet. And write the relevant qualifications and training that you possess on the right.

Outcomes and achievements

Finally, take a look back at Chapter 2 to list the outcomes that you think this particular employer wants to achieve. List those outcomes on the left side of a sheet of paper. On the right side of the sheet, write down the achievements you have accomplished that demonstrate your ability to deliver those outcomes.

Again, in filling out the right-hand column, consider that your achievements may have been accomplished in either your paid or unpaid work, as well as your professional or personal life.

Investing to succeed

You may be reading this and thinking, Yes, it would be nice to do some research and tailor every CV I send out – but I don't have the time. Be careful. You're at risk of falling into a very, very big trap. Granted, sending out the same CV to more than one employer will save you time. But it's a false economy. Because you're almost certain not to get invited to an interview.

When most job adverts receive so many applications, you can be guaranteed that someone else will have spent time carefully researching the organization and tailoring their CV to make them seem like the perfect candidate. Against that kind of competition, a standard CV just doesn't stand much of a chance.

Taking an hour to send out one tailored, carefully targeted CV is a better use of your time than sending out a dozen more-or-less identical CVs. You have been warned!

Rookie Buster

Taking an hour to send out one tailored, carefully targeted CV is a better use of your time than sending out a dozen more-or-less identical CVs.

48 *Creating your profile statement*

Your name goes at the top of your CV. Then the next bit of your CV to write is a *profile statement*. Sometimes also called a "career objective" or an "asset statement", a profile statement is a short (one to five sentence long) paragraph at the top of your CV announcing who you are and how your strengths and achievements can help an employer. Here are a handful of examples:

A help desk operative with a confident telephone manner and outstanding knowledge of PC systems and remote working. I am customer-focused and have a reputation of exceeding callers' expectations when they need talking through on computer-related issues.

Human resources professional with responsibility for looking after an internal customer base of 500 employees. Experienced in projects relating to: recruitment and selection, leadership development, staff development, compensation and benefits. Managed one human resources assistant. Interacted frequently with senior managers to deliver successful human resources initiatives.

I graduated with an upper second class degree in history and economics. I have experience of working in several office environments. In order to pursue a career in marketing, I recently spent two weeks on an internship at Molloy & Channing.

Your profile statement plays an important role, enabling employers to figure out immediately why they should pay attention to the rest of your CV. But bear in mind that employers are not interested in what you want. You must summarize what you can offer an employer. So never tell them what kind of work you are looking for. Always tell them about your experience, skills, knowledge or the outcomes you have delivered that will help your target employer to succeed in its goals.

Rookie Buster

Your profile statement plays an important role, enabling employers to figure out immediately why they should pay attention to the rest of your CV.

Deciding on the right format for you

The first decision you make – before you write a single word of your CV – is the format that will best showcase your talents and experience.

The traditional way to lay out your CV is to list your employment and education details in a *reverse chronological* format. In other words, you list your most recent employment, followed by your previous job, the one before that, and so on. Then you do the same for your education, listing your most recent qualifications or schooling and then going backwards in time.

However, the reverse chronological format does not suit everyone. So instead many people choose to adopt a *skills-based* (also called a "functional") format for their CV instead. Let's look at examples, and the pros and cons of each.

Reverse chronological format

On the next page you'll see the basic layout of a reverse chronological CV.

[YOUR NAME]

Address, city, postcode

Telephone numbers; email address

EXPERIENCE

20** – present Job title, Employer's name, Employer's location

A brief paragraph (two to a maximum of five sentences) on your role in the organization, including details of your key responsibilities.

- Your most impressive achievement in this role (that is relevant to *this particular* employer).
- Your second most impressive and relevant achievement.
- Your third most impressive achievement.

20**–20**   Job title, Employer's name, Employer's location

(Repeat as for your current job)

19**–20**   Job title, Employer's name, Employer's location

(Repeat as for your current job)

Etc.

EDUCATION AND TRAINING

List here in reverse date order (in other words, most recent ones first) your most impressive qualifications, training courses attended, professional memberships, degrees and so on.

In listing your achievements, remember to lead with the most impressive and relevant information *for that particular employer*. I can't stress this point enough. What impresses one employer may not impress the next. And consider the advantages and disadvantages of the reverse chronological format:

Pros

- The most popular way to set out your experience and education.
- The format confirms the continuity of your experience, such as that you have had 8, 10 or 20 years' unbroken experience in a field or profession.

Cons

- The reverse chronological format does not suit people who are trying to change from one field of work to another (for example, from one occupation to another, from military service into commercial work, from one sector into another, etc.).
- This format can expose periods of unemployment.
- This format can expose the fact that you don't have very much work experience.
- This format can expose the fact that you didn't stay long in your previous roles.

Skills-based format

The skills-based format focuses the reader's attention on how you meet the requirements for the role (rather than on your actual employment history). On the next page you'll see the basic layout of a skills-based CV.

[YOUR NAME]
Address, city, postcode
Telephone numbers; email address

SKILLS/ACHIEVEMENTS
Your top skill (in other words, the one that is most relevant and impressive to *this particular* employer).

- Your most impressive achievement, illustrating how you used this skill to deliver a positive outcome for an organization.
- Your next most impressive achievement.

Your second top skill.

- (Repeat as per your top skill.)

Your third top skill.

- (Repeat as per your top skill.)

Your fourth top skill (if necessary).

- (Repeat as per your top skill.)

EXPERIENCE

20**–Present	Job title, Employer's name and location
20**–20**	Job title, Employer's name and location
20**–20**	Job title, Employer's name and location
Etc.	

EDUCATION AND TRAINING
Summarize very briefly your qualifications, degrees or other education.

Again, you may need to choose to highlight different skills to impress different employers. And here are the pros and cons of using a skill-based format:

Pros

- You can direct the reader's attention to how you are right for the job rather than the fact that you may not have the traditional background and employment history that he or she is expecting.
- You repeat back to the employer exactly the key skills (based on your reading of the job advert and research) that the organization is looking for.
- You can downplay work experience that is not entirely relevant to the kind of work you are now looking for.

Cons

- Experienced employers can sometimes be suspicious of CVs that do not list your employment history first. As such, the reader may assume that you are hiding something such as inappropriate work experience or educational failings.
- A skills-based format may not make the most of your employment history if you have worked for companies that are household names within your industry.

Rookie Buster

In listing your achievements, remember to lead with the most impressive and relevant information *for that particular employer.*

Making the right choice of format

The reverse chronological format may hamper you if you are looking to do something that is different from what you have done in the past. Say you are a receptionist, but now want to become a teacher. Or a bank manager, but want to retrain as a veterinary nurse. Listing your relevant skills in a skills-based format may be the better choice for you.

54   The skills-based format may also be better for you if you are a recent graduate or school leaver with little or no work experience. You can talk about how you have demonstrated the right skills in your studies and unpaid experiences.

And the skills-based format can help candidates with significant gaps in their career history (for instance due to unemployment or illness) or "job hoppers" who may be perceived by employers as lacking commitment.

So which format is going to suit you best?

Capturing your contact details

OK, let's get started on the next section of your CV. Always begin with your name at the top (you don't need to say "Curriculum Vitae" or "CV", as it is obvious enough what the document is) and personal profile. Then most CVs include certain contact details. And here's how they should be set out:

TERESA HOLLINS

Marketing manager with 10 years' experience of working with branded consumer goods. I lead and coach a team of five people. Having originally trained as an accountant, I have a firm grasp of numbers and am focused on helping the business to create value for shareholders.

[Your profile statement should take up the first 3 to 5 sentences here.]

Address: Flat 7, 5th Floor, 11 Carrington Road, Birmingham B99 8ZP
Phone: 0191 7891 5476
Mobile: 07911 3021 6481
Email: thollins2000@googlemail.com

Now, that looks simple enough, right? A couple of pointers, though:

- Make sure that if you give your home telephone number, you have an answering machine or answering service to record calls if you cannot answer the telephone yourself. And consider getting a separate, cheap, pay-as-you-call mobile phone if you don't have one already, so that you will know that any calls you receive on that phone are of the utmost importance.
- Include a personal email address rather than the one you currently use for your work. Employers are legally permitted to check that your work email is being used only for work purposes – you could find yourself fired if your employer finds you using your work email address to look for a new job!
- And use a sensible email address. Avoid "doctor_spanky@emailaddress.net" or "sexy.chick@emailprovider.com", as some employers might object to such supposedly humorous email addresses.
- Do *not* include your marital status or the number of children you have. I have never met a single employer who has ever thought "Oh, this person is married and has two children – I must give her the job!"

Avoiding the seven deadly sins of writing your CV

There are many myths about what constitutes a winning CV. Be sure to avoid the following fatal flaws when pulling together your CV.

Sin 1: Being too verbose

Keep your CV short! Your CV should whet the reader's appetite to find out more about you; you should not be aiming to inundate the employer with absolutely everything that can be said about you.

As a rule of thumb, keep your CV to one page if you have five or fewer years' paid work experience. If you are more experienced, feel free to have two pages. Only if you have substantial (i.e. 10+ years), directly relevant experience should you stretch to three pages. Anything more than three pages merely tells the employer that you are a long-winded person who struggles to be concise.

Sin 2: Making pompous claims about yourself

It's fine to talk about skills such as influencing people or analysing problems. And it's good to mention achievements such as the actual results you have attained. But steer clear of describing yourself using phrases such as "an ambitious worker with an optimistic, supportive and helpful attitude" or "a talented, warm individual with management potential".

Be very careful of using empty adjectives. Strong candidates avoid adjectives entirely and instead give brief examples to *prove* that they have the right skills.

Sin 3: Delving into the distant past

Focus the reader on your *recent* employment history. An employer is most interested in what you have been doing in the last five to ten years. If you have more than ten years' experience, summarize your early days rather than giving them too much space on your CV. Perhaps include a heading on "Experience" for your most recent few years, and then another heading below that entitled "Experience prior to 1999" (or whatever year you choose) and condense anything that is less recent.

This point is especially important if you feel that you may have too much experience (for example, if you are sure that most of the other applicants for the job may be considerably younger). Try this tactic also if you have the wrong sort of experience (for instance if you spent the first few years of your career doing the "wrong" job before you

changed into the "right" one for you) for a job and need to gloss over
some of your earlier work details.

Rookie Buster

An employer is most interested in what you have been doing in the last five to ten years.

Sin 4: Including irrelevant information

You will notice that I have not included a section on either the reverse chronological or skills-based CV formats for sections such as "extra-curricular activities" or "hobbies and interests". And that's because, for most people, including such a section adds nothing to a CV.

I realize that many job hunters want to add information to their CVs to show that they have lives outside their work. But employers don't care. The truth is that employers are more interested in how you can use your skills and experience to help them succeed than they are in your life outside work. So include extracurricular activities *only* if they are relevant *and* impactful *and* recent.

For instance, if you are applying for a job in marketing, then mentioning that you "attend regular conferences and seminars of the National Institute of Marketing and Communications" may strengthen your application. But mentioning that you "play the guitar in spare time", "read books and go to the cinema" or "spend time with my family" isn't going to impress an employer.

Similarly, do mention if you play a team sport (as employers sometimes believe that people who play team sports are better team players at work). But don't mention it if the last time you played a team sport was more than five years ago – because that just makes it sound as if you haven't done anything worthwhile in the last five years!

58

Rookie Buster

Include extracurricular activities *only* if they are relevant *and* impactful *and* recent.

Sin 5: Providing too much information

Never share the reasons you left your past jobs *unless you are specifically asked to do so*. You may need to answer questions about why you left your current or previous jobs during a job interview, but you do *not* need to mention your reasons, even in passing, on a CV.

Whether you're currently employed, have just been made redundant, or have been out of work for some time, you should not include such information. The vast majority of job hunters do not share such information on their CVs. So choosing to include such information on your CV can therefore raise suspicions about your loyalty in the mind of an employer. Focus instead on the skills, achievements and experience that you can offer to help the potential employer with its goals.

In fact, strip out all shortcomings, negative information or tales of adversity on your CV. So if you have been ill or have suffered family difficulties, or anything else – do *not* mention it on your CV. Remember that a CV is a sales document – it is designed to promote your best skills and attributes.

And avoid mentioning your current salary or salary requirements *unless the employer specifically asks for it* too. The danger of mentioning it on your CV is that if you are too expensive, you will immediately be eliminated from consideration. By not mentioning it, you may be able to meet the interviewers and impress them so much in person that they could raise the maximum salary they are willing to pay.

Sin 6: Going crazy with the design of your CV   59

Your CV must be a professional-looking document. So bear in mind the following pointers:

- Use sheets of standard-sized plain white paper for printing out your CV. Coloured paper, especially thick paper, or paper of an unusual shape or size only annoys the person trying to file it.
- Choose a simple typeface such as Helvetica or Times Roman. And use the standard font size that your word processing program uses as its default. Avoid shrinking the font size to squeeze more on to your CV – experienced employers immediately spot this as the tactic of a desperate job hunter who can't prioritize what to include on a CV.
- Use the standard settings for the margins, headers and footers of your CV too. Avoid reducing them to squash more content on to your CV. Choosing carefully what to include on your CV to sell your talents will make a better impression than trying to cram as much as you can on to the printed page.
- Be careful of trying to impress an employer through gimmicks. Very few employers appreciate gimmicks, such as jokes printed on CVs, and most experienced employers have seen them all before.

Sin 7: Making spelling or grammatical mistakes

There really is no excuse for having either spelling or grammatical errors on your CV. Any errors on your CV immediately raise questions in the mind of the reader about your attention to detail (or your lack of it).

60   One of the problems is that you get so used to looking at your own CV that your brain stops looking for mistakes. To make sure you side-step this sin, work your way through these three steps:

1. Use the spell checker on your computer to check for common spelling mistakes.

2. Print out your CV and read through it line by line. By the time you have worked on your CV a few times, your eyes may get used to ignoring mistakes on a computer screen. Print it out and read through it line by line, covering up the rest of the CV with a ruler or sheet of paper. S-l-o-w down and you may spot errors that you overlooked on screen.

3. Print out your CV and give it to a friend or two to read. Explain to your friends that you would appreciate it if they could point out any errors or even sentences that do not make immediate sense.

Coach's notes

- Tailor your CV. Yes, it does take longer to write a CV that perfectly meets the needs of a particular vacancy. But given that there will be other job hunters who are tailoring their CVs, any CV of yours that does not perfectly meet the brief will almost certainly end up in the discard pile.
- Write a profile statement by carefully choosing 1 to 5 sentences to explain how your skills and achievements can help a potential employer to meet its goals. But remember that the profile statement you use for one job may differ subtly from the one you use for another job.
- Consider the pros and cons of a reverse chronological versus a skills-based format for your CV. The reverse chronological format demonstrates your continuity of experience. The skills-based format demonstrates your skills and achievements even if you may not have exactly the background and career history that the employer is expecting to see.
- Keep the rest of your CV simple. When considering whether to include a particular piece of information about anything – your education, your marital status, your hobbies and interests, and so on – always make sure that it is relevant *and* impactful *and* recent.

Go for it! Always, always, always write your CV with employers in mind. Remember that you should include the kind of information that employers want to hear – not the stuff that you want to mention! And think about the order of information so that your most impressive stuff hits the reader straight away. Do that, and you give yourself the best shot at getting invited along to an interview.

Notes

A strong CV must be more than just a factual summary of your skills and achievements. A strong CV has to be a summary of the *right* skills and achievements. In this chapter, I show you how to choose the right words and phrases - in both your CV and the covering letter you may have to write - to sell yourself to the employer.

CHAPTER 4

Sending your CV to the next level

Incorporating winning words and persuasive phrases

I warned in Chapter 3 (page 56) that adjectives tend to be perceived by employers as pompous and empty. However, the right *verbs* can help to lift your CV in an employer's estimation. Employers increasingly want to read about not only *what* you achieved, but also *how* you achieved it.

Compare the following examples:

Achievement on its own = good
- Improved customer satisfaction within the branch.
- Increased sales by 14 per cent.

Achievement plus *how* you achieved it = better
- Conducted a survey to measure customer satisfaction and identified a number of "quick wins" to improve customer satisfaction within the branch.

66 • Increased sales by 14 per cent by gathering the team together for a brainstorming session, reviewing the best ideas to turn into a strategy, and then coaching the team to achieve our new strategy.

As you can see, explaining the steps you took to complete your achievements makes you sound more credible.

Rookie Buster

Employers increasingly want to read about not only *what* you achieved, but also *how* you achieved it.

Using achievement-oriented verbs

Here are three categories of verbs that you may wish to use in describing the steps you took to deliver your achievements. Bear in mind that these are only *examples* – there are thousands more verbs in the English language! And also do look back at the list of verbs in the exercise: 'Self-Discovery 1: Understanding your skills' (in Chapter 1, page 12).

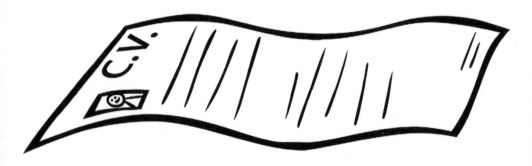

Working with data and ideas

Analysed	Edited	Interpreted
Calculated	Eliminated	Outlined
Communicated	Evaluated	Programmed
Compared	Explained	Recommended
Compiled	Forecasted	Researched
Decided	Formulated	Reviewed
Developed	Generated	Solved

Working with people

Advised	Helped	Negotiated
Coached	Influenced	Persuaded
Collaborated	Instructed	Recruited
Consulted	Led	Served
Counselled	Listened (to)	Supervised
Discussed	Mentored	Taught
Guided	Motivated	Trained

Working with projects and things

Assembled	Handled	Purchased
Bought	Increased	Reduced
Budgeted	Inspected	Repaired
Built	Invented	Scheduled
Constructed	Managed	Sold
Coordinated	Ordered	Solved (a problem)
Delivered	Planned	Tested

Choosing the right verbs for you

Remember that those three lists are *examples* of the kinds of verbs you may wish to include on your CV. There are countless other verbs that may be more appropriate to your occupation or field of expertise.

And remember to include a particular verb only if you believe both that you possess it and it is directly relevant to the role and therefore attractive to the employer. Organizations spend a lot of time agonizing

68 over the right words for their job adverts in an attempt to capture the values and culture of their businesses. You must avoid including a particular word or phrase if you are merely proud of having that skill!

For example, you may have a fantastic typing speed of 90 words per minute. But if the job does not require fast typing, you could *reduce* your attractiveness to an employer by mentioning it because the employer may think you're wrong for the job. Or if you have great experience of leading teams, be careful not to dwell on it too much on your CV if the next job you are looking for is a technical role with little opportunity for leadership.

Putting your skills into action

Write in the first person (not the third person, which makes you sound self-important), but omit the pronoun. Simply start with a verb. For example, "Managed a team of 3 juniors" (rather than "I managed a team of 3 juniors").

When writing about your skills and achievements, make sure you start all of your sentences with a verb. Avoid starting some with a verb and some with a noun. Compare the following:

Sentences starting with verbs and nouns = bad
- "Developed new process for streamlining manufacturing efficiency. Cost reduction of 3.2 per cent over target."
- "Founder of own business. Generated £60,000 of sales in first year."

Sentences starting only with verbs = good
- "Developed new process for streamlining manufacturing efficiency. Achieved cost reduction of 3.2 per cent over target."
- "Founded own business. Generated £60,000 of sales in first year."

Use the past tense for jobs that you have left and the present tense for a job you are still in. So you "managed 2 teaching assistants" in your previous job, but currently "manage a team of 3 teaching assistants and 2 teachers".

And avoid the passive tense (for example, "Team was restructured   69
for greater efficiency") and write in the active voice instead (for
example, "Restructured team for greater efficiency"). The active voice
sounds more action-oriented and compelling.

Rookie Buster

When writing about your skills and achievements,
make sure you start all of your sentences with a verb.

Combining skills and results to create your achievements

Your CV will always be more attractive if you talk about the results you
achieved rather than the responsibilities you held. So quantify the
results you achieved. If possible, mention numbers, percentages and
money. Because there's nothing like helping employers to see pound,
dollar or euro signs when they read your CV.

So rather than throwing lots of action verbs on to your CV, ensure
you make the connection for the reader by giving specific examples of
the results you achieved. *What* did you manage or improve? *What* did
you design or launch?

Have a look back at "Understanding organizational goals" in
Chapter 2 (on page 31). And consider these examples:

- Increased sales by 28 per cent.
- Completed a project that reduced wastage by 3 per cent.
- Improved our health and safety record.
- Devised a new way of working that reduced costs, saving £1,200
  over the course of the year.
- Achieved a 96 per cent attendance record (as compared with the
  company average of 89 per cent).

70
- Was ranked 3rd best sales person within the team of 14 sales people.
- Enhanced customer satisfaction, with 8 in 10 customers now ranking us as "excellent" in their dealings with us.
- Reduced complaints from around 10 a week to fewer than 3 a week.
- Brought the project in on time and under budget.
- Increased productivity by 45 per cent over 3 years.
- Recruited, trained, and coached 3 new members of the team.

Rookie Buster

Talk about the results you achieved rather than the responsibilities you held.

What other results and positive outcomes do you think the kinds of organizations you want to work for are looking for?

Telling a coherent story

Your CV is a sales document and needs to position you as the best person for *both* the specific role (such as accountant, teacher, managing director) *and* the particular organization you are applying for. Be sure to select only the experience, skills, achievements and education that tell a compelling story about why you fit the brief for both the role and the organization.

In creating your CV, include *only what is impressive and relevant.* I've already mentioned this, but it's so important that it's worth mentioning again! Including information that is not impressive or immediately relevant may dilute the strength of your application.

You do *not* have to include everything for the sake of completeness. 71
For example, you may have great computer programming skills. But if
the job does not relate to computers or technology, don't bring them
up. Or if you started your career working in retail but now want to
change direction and work in public relations, mention only the skills
and achievements that help to paint a picture of you as a competent
public relations person.

Rookie Buster

In creating your CV, include *only what is impressive and relevant.*

Bringing it all together

Over the page are a couple of examples of CVs that incorporate all of
the points we have covered so far. Compare the similarities and differ-
ences between the reverse chronological format and the skills-based
format.

Remember that the reverse chronological format is best for you if
you have an established track record in one field. In the example on
page 72, the candidate (Leslie Mitchell) is already a web designer and
is applying for a further job in web design.

Remember that a skills-based CV may be better for you if you have
a non-traditional background or are trying to change career. In the
example on page 73, the candidate (Chris Owen) may want to move
away from retail into a different line of work, such as working as a
manager in a new field.

Example of reverse chronological CV

LESLIE MITCHELL

Web designer with experience of working with clients ranging from small owner-managed businesses to large corporations. Proven track record of delivering projects on time, under budget and to clients' specifications.

Flat 18, Morningside Mansions, 38 Armstrong Avenue, London, MM7 TK8.
Telephone: 0171 1808 1295. Mobile: 09103 432 9133.
Email: lesliemitchell_uk@hotmail.com

EXPERIENCE

2007–present   Senior Web Designer, Momentum Design Creations, London. Using Flex, Flash, Photoshop, Illustrator, Dreamweaver (plus PHP, MySQL, XML, HTML, CSS) to meet client needs. Key achievements include:
- Working with Boston First Bank (of the USA) to build www.bostonfirstbank.co.uk to launch their UK business. Managed a team of 3 designers and liaised extensively with client to deliver project on time, on budget and to their complete satisfaction.
- Creating a new concept for health company Go Banana and building an online shop for sale of their products both in UK and internationally.

2005–2007   Web Designer, Apollo Concepts, London. Key achievements include:
- Re-designing website for charity PetCare International – meeting the client's demanding specification on an extremely tight budget.
- Building a new corporate website for British Metals in only 3 months.
- Creating the concept for architecture firm Hass & Friedman's new website and building it entirely in Flash.

2002–2005   Web Designer, Allen & Company. Key achievements include:
- Creating new logo and design identity for Cornfield Insurance.
- Building banner ads for clients including Gartmore TV, PharmaZone, and Computer Magic.

EDUCATION

2001–2002   1-year diploma in multimedia design and technology.
2000   A Levels in IT (A), Physics (B), Maths (C).

Example of skills-based CV   73

CHRIS OWEN

Experienced manager with track record of meeting or exceeding sales targets. Strong coaching skills and ability to take new hires and turn them into confident and sales-focused employees.

173 Portland Terrace, Manchester, MM7 TK8.
Telephone: 0113 8790 1256. Mobile: 08911 871 8955.
Email: c.owen1234@googlemail.com

SKILLS/ACHIEVEMENTS
SALES FOCUS
- Hit or exceeded my sales targets in 10 of the last 12 months.
- In a previous role, ensured we exceeded quarterly sales targets for winter season promotions in 3 consecutive years.
- Arranged a 'First Thursday' monthly author visit and signing evening, which boosted sales on those Thursdays by at least 20 per cent.

COACHING AND DEVELOPING TEAMS
- Interviewed and brought on board 12 new members of staff in current role. Coached and trained new members of staff in sales techniques and provision of customer care.
- Allocated work and managed the entire store (of 32 staff) in absence of the general manager.

FINANCIAL AND COMMERCIAL SKILLS
- Prepared monthly financial reports for head office to ensure good financial management.
- Conducted a stock profitability project that identified which products we should remove from the store and what new ones to bring in.

PROJECT MANAGEMENT
- Worked with external IT supplier to implement successfully a computerized stock tracking system – the system has now been rolled out across all Wonder Books stores.

EXPERIENCE
2008–present Senior Assistant Store Manager, Computer World, Croydon.
2005–2008   Assistant Store Manager, Wonder Books, London.
2004–2005   Customer Service Associate, Wonder Books, London.

EDUCATION/TRAINING
2006   Week-long management training course (Computer World).
2001–2004   B.Sc. English and Politics, West London University.
2000   A Levels in English, History, French.

74 *Writing effective covering letters*

Most people understand that it's common practice to send a covering letter to an employer together with your CV. And there are good reasons to write a compelling covering letter:

- A well-written and carefully crafted covering letter allows you to draw the reader's attention to the key aspects of your CV that make you an attractive candidate.
- A well-researched covering letter demonstrates that you want the job badly enough to have taken the time to find out more about the organization than other candidates.

So the first and most important point to make about writing an effective covering letter is that *you must always tailor it.* Sending out CVs to random employers does not work. If you've gone to all the effort of tailoring a CV, you must also tailor a covering letter that tells the reader exactly why you are perfect for the job at *their* organization. Anything else just isn't good enough.

As an employer myself, I receive job applications from people who want to work at my company, Talentspace. They say things like "Having researched your company, I believe I am a perfect fit." Yet they don't *demonstrate* what they know about Talentspace by telling me what they have uncovered in their research. I honestly cannot recall a single covering letter that has ever referred to a client that Talentspace has worked with, an article written by myself or a colleague, or anything that could *prove* that they actually did any research. Despite the fact that they have addressed their letters to Talentspace, their letters appear no more focused than if they had been sent out entirely at random.

So the lesson is: you are better off doing *at least* a half-hour (or more) of in-depth research on a particular organization and only sending off one letter than sending out a dozen letters with only the name and address of the company changed in each letter.

Example: covering letter

Note that an effective covering letter should only be a single page in length. Here's an example of a covering letter, written by Chris Owen to accompany the CV on page 73.

173 Portland Terrace
Manchester MM7 TK8

(Date)
Jamie Peterson
Regional Manager
Nova Bank
Molton Business Park
Moltonshire MJ3 P8L

Dear Mr Peterson,

I read with great interest your recent advert in *The Financial Post* for bank branch managers. In the light of Nova's stated strategy of recruiting people with customer service experience rather than necessarily banking backgrounds, I believe I am well suited for the position as I have considerable experience of having delivered outstanding sales results in two different environments.

When I took my on current role at the Croydon branch of Computer World, the store had failed to hit its sales targets for 6 of the past 9 months. However, I have recruited new staff and coached them in how to care for customers such that our store has actually met or *exceeded* its sales targets in 10 of the last 12 months.

I already take on many of the responsibilities of a store manager when the general manager is absent from Computer World. For example, when he took a 2-week holiday, I took sole responsibility for the smooth running of the store – from sorting out the team's rosters and shift patterns to re-ordering stock and resolving supplier and customer issues successfully.

I would very much like the opportunity to meet with you in person and tell you more about how I can contribute to helping Nova to achieve its ambition of becoming one of the country's top ten banks. I look forward to hearing from you soon.

Yours sincerely,

Chris Owen

OK, now let's take each section of the covering letter and talk through how you can make it work for you.

Addressing your letter

Letter-writing convention dictates that you should include the name and address of the person you are writing to in the following sequence:

Line 1:   The person's full name (if you know it)
Line 2:   The person's job title (if you know it)
Line 3:   The department (use department if you don't have the person's job title)
Line 4:   Name of the organization
Line 5:   Street name and address
Line 6:   City and postcode

Here's a worked example:

Mrs Hilary Tomlinson
Sales & Marketing Manager
Pet Products Trading
181 Gulliver Place
Luton LS77 JTM

Dear Mrs Tomlinson

Do your best to find out the name and job title of the person you should be writing to. Telephone the organization's switchboard and simply ask for the name and job title of the person who is responsible for the recruitment of that particular role. I'm much more likely to pay attention to a job hunter who has taken the trouble to find out my name rather than simply addressing the letter to "The Managing Director at Talentspace". Job hunters who choose to use broad umbrella terms create the impression that they can't be bothered to find out my name. And check carefully the spelling of the name and the organization.

However, if you can't get a name and job title, you may need to start the letter with the salutation: "To whom it may concern".

Writing your opening paragraph

Your first paragraph serves two purposes:
- It should announce the reason you are getting in touch (in other words, that you are either responding to a specific job advert or writing speculatively to the organization).
- It should grab the reader's attention and give them a compelling reason for wanting to read on.

One of the best ways to grab the reader's attention is by making a connection between yourself and the person you're writing to. Consider these examples:
- "I'm writing to you at the suggestion of our mutual friend, Lindsay Brown, who mentioned that you are looking for a new sales manager."
- "I met your colleague David Green at the ICGM Conference in Leeds; he suggested that I get in touch to see if there might be an opportunity for me to join the team."
- "I am contacting you on the recommendation of Tom White, who felt that someone with my skills and experience might be able to add value to your team."

Of course, in order to make a connection, you must be able to mention the name of someone that the reader both knows *and* respects. No point mentioning the name of someone that the reader knows but can't stand!

The person whose name you mention does not have to be a close personal friend of yours. That person could be someone you know only casually, perhaps having met them briefly at a conference or party. But so long as you get that person's permission to use his or her name, you will help your covering letter to stand out from the rest of the crowd. We'll discuss how to get the names of people in Chapter 5: Enlisting support for your job hunt.

An alternative is to demonstrate your in-depth knowledge of the organization. Your goal here is to mention a fact or observation about the organization that is not common knowledge, in order to show the reader that you are committed enough to have done some research. Here are a few examples:

- "I am responding to your recent advertisement in *The Daily Chronicle*. As your company is now moving from print media into radio broadcasting, I believe I am ideally placed (having had 6 years' experience in radio production) to contribute to the sustained growth of the company."

- "I have been following with great interest the growth and success of your business since it expanded into the UK. I am getting in touch as the reputable financial press has reported that you are likely to open an office in Germany within the next year. As a fluent German speaker and a graduate in marketing, I believe I am ideally placed to help the continued expansion of your business."

Telling the employer what you offer

The second and third paragraphs of your letter should tell the employer how you can help to make the organization more successful. You should *not* talk about what you want; focus only on what you can offer.

As you write these paragraphs, remember, remember, remember to write about how you can help the employer. So choose your two best examples of how you have helped your current or previous employers to achieve their organizational goals. You may want to highlight certain skills, pertinent technical expertise, past achievements or even the length of your experience – so long as you believe that it illustrates how you can help the reader's organization.

Your best example should form the first paragraph; your second best example should form the second paragraph. If you believe that you have a vitally important third example, you may wish to use three, rather than two, paragraphs to tell the employer what you can offer.

Rookie Buster

Remember, remember, remember to write about how you can help the employer.

Compare these examples that talk about what the job hunter wants versus what the job hunter can offer:

Talking about what you want = bad
- "I have always wanted to work in the advertising industry."
- "Children's Hope is one of the country's leading charities and I know that I would enjoy working on projects that benefit children's welfare."

Talking about what you can offer = good
- "Having written several extended essays during my course work on the tools that companies use to create effective television adverts, I believe I am well placed to pursue a career in advertising."
- "In recent months I have been working part-time for several non-profit groups and now have a strong understanding of the needs of the non-profit sector. I also have considerable experience of working in public relations – for example having launched over a dozen new products in the last 3 years – so would be able to contribute significantly towards raising the profile of Children's Hope."

Closing your letter

To end the letter, most job hunters choose two or three sentences to convey their hope that they will be invited to interview. Take a look at these examples:
- "Please get in touch if you have any questions about my background or how I have helped my previous employers to

80 achieve their organizational goals. I appreciate your consideration and would be most grateful for the chance for us to meet in person."

- "I would welcome the opportunity to meet with you in person or to speak over the telephone. I look forward to hearing from you soon."

Finally, to sign off your letter, "Yours sincerely" followed by your name (plus your signature between the two if you are sending an actual physical letter as opposed to an email) is ideal. If you do not have a name for the person you are addressing (for example, if you are addressing the letter "To whom it may concern"), you can use "Yours faithfully".

Getting your CV in front of an employer

Once you are happy with the content of your CV and covering letter, be sure to *follow the instructions carefully for sending them to the employer*. For example, an employer could possibly ask you to send *two* copies of your CV in the post instead of the more usual one copy. Be sure to print them on clean sheets of paper – no mucky smudges or crumpled corners!

If you are emailing it, make sure you use a fully formatted version in Microsoft Word. If you're worried about having an older or incompatible version of word processing software, look online for free tools that allow you to create documents with the .pdf extension so you can be certain that your documents will appear on the employer's screen precisely in the way that you intend them to look.

Coach's notes

- Scan the job advert and try to use as many relevant achievement-oriented verbs to explain not only what you achieved but also how you achieved it. However, remember to mention skills only if they are directly relevant to the job – including other skills that are less relevant can actually distract the reader and dilute the strength of your CV.
- Quantify the results you achieved wherever possible. Numbers, percentages and money are the best ways to impress employers that you are someone who can help them to achieve their organizational goals.
- Check that your CV tells a coherent story. Once you have finished the draft of your CV, check that you have included only the information that is both relevant *and* impressive.
- Tailor your covering letter in the same way as you tailor your CV. The covering letter you write to one employer may need to be quite different from the letter you write to another employer.
- Remember that your covering letter should be used to highlight and expand upon the two (or three) achievements or skills that you believe are the *most* impressive from your CV.

Go for it! Turn a good CV into a great one. Tailor your CV and write a covering letter that perfectly meets the specific needs of each and every employer. And remember that your covering letter must explain how you can help the employer – not what you want. Make this investment in every application and you can expect to get invited along for an interview very soon.

Notes

Surveys show that *between 50 and 85 per cent of vacancies* are filled by word of mouth. Yes, that's a lot of people finding jobs through the people that they know. Other people are probably your greatest resource when it comes to finding a new job. And in this chapter, I show you how you can ask your friends for their support, find new acquaintances, and track down the job you want.

CHAPTER 5

Enlisting support for your job hunt

Understanding the facts about networking

Networking is simply about talking to people. By picking up the telephone, sending out the occasional email and meeting people in person, you serve two purposes:

1. You can ask people for advice, information and referrals to other people who might be able to help you find a job or point you in the right direction of job-leads.
2. You raise your profile and remind people that you exist! People can't recommend you for jobs or tell you about job-leads if they forget that you are looking for a new job.

That's all that networking involves. In fact, this is possibly the most important chapter in this book, so please take note! And here are five important facts about networking.

Rookie Buster

Between *50 and 85 per cent of vacancies* are filled by word of mouth.

Fact 1: Networking is simply about talking to people

Networking is simply a fancy word for getting in touch with people and asking for their help. For example, say a friend of yours (let's call her Christina Jenkins) suggests that you speak to a friend of hers (let's call him Stephen Birtwell). You might then phone Stephen up and say: "Hi, Christina Jenkins gave me your number and said that you might be able to help. Do you have a few minutes to talk on the phone?"

That's all networking involves. All you need to do is pick up the telephone or send an email mentioning the name of someone you know. Pretty straight-forward, right?

The good news when it comes to networking is that you don't need to know anyone important. We are all connected to a network of friends, family members, ex-colleagues, and acquaintances. And, for the most part, they are all willing to help us.

Rookie Buster

Networking is simply a fancy word for getting in touch with people and asking for their help.

Fact 2: Employers often prefer not to advertise   87

You may be wondering why so many jobs are filled by word of mouth. Many employers find that the payback simply isn't good enough to justify the cost of an advert in the press or online. And some employers prefer not to advertise because they find that candidates who come to them by way of word-of-mouth referrals tend to be of a higher calibre than those who respond to job adverts.

Fact 3: Networking generates better quality job opportunities

Networking not only opens up a greater *quantity* of jobs but also a better *quality* of job vacancies too. The best jobs are often filled by someone who knows someone who knows someone. People are much more likely to recommend a job to their friends and contacts when the role is interesting and the pay is good.

It's often the less desirable jobs that end up getting advertised. So networking is a much more successful technique for job hunting than relying on recruitment consultants or online job websites.

Fact 4: People are usually happy to help

I can understand if you feel a bit unsure about the idea of having to get in touch with people. But trust me when I say that the vast majority of people are usually only too happy to help.

If someone rang you and told you that a mutual friend had recommended you as an expert in your field, wouldn't you be able to spare them 15 minutes of your time? I would. And I often do!

So long as you phrase your request in the right way (which we shall come on to later in this chapter), you will almost certainly find that most people are very willing to share their ideas and advice.

88 *Getting ready to network*

You need to take two steps before picking up the telephone.

1: Listing your contacts

The good news is that the first step is very easy. Begin by listing all of the people you know – yes, *everyone*. Take a sheet of paper and jot down the names of everyone you can think of.

Consider the names of current and previous colleagues, customers and clients, suppliers, people you know through professional or voluntary associations. Think about accountants, lawyers, web designers, and any other advisers or consultants you may have used or come across. Think also about your life outside work – what about people from social, community, sporting or religious organizations? How about people from school or university, military service, even neighbours, and of course family too?

You may be tempted to shorten this brainstorming process. You may believe that certain people will be more useful than others – and you're right. But bear in mind that family and close friends may be more *likely* to want to help – even if they can't point you immediately in the direction of your dream job.

Keep scribbling until your list hits *at least* 200 people. Once you're done, you can prioritize the names based on two criteria:

- *Likely usefulness.* An ex-colleague who works in the same field as you may be more influential or better connected than a colleague who worked in a different department. Or a friend who is in charge of a department may have more contacts than another friend who is just starting out in his career.
- *Strength of relationship.* A close friend is probably more willing to spare the time and enthusiasm to listen to you and coach and advise you than someone you see as more of an acquaintance.

To prioritize your list of names, draw up a simple table, copy across the names from your list, and allocate between one and three stars to

each name depending on how you rate their likely helpfulness. Then
allocate between one and three ticks to each name based on the strength
of your relationship with them. Here's an example:

Name	Usefulness	Relationship
Holly Kennedy	★ ★	✓
Parminder Singh	★	✓ ✓
Mary Tsoi	★	✓ ✓
Richard Jefferson	★ ★ ★	✓ ✓ ✓

2: Writing your networking script

Nearly time to pick up the telephone. But before you do, you may want
to figure out what you want to say. You need to introduce yourself (and
your request) in a professional, yet friendly manner.

I strongly recommend that you write out – at least in draft form –
what you want to say in the form of a networking script. Try to cover
the following points:

1. A single sentence describing your profession or the type of work
    you do.
2. Mention of how you got this person's name. For example: "I spoke
    to your ex-colleague, Catherine Wallace, who suggested that you
    wouldn't mind taking a call from me."
3. Your current situation, and what this person could do for you. For
    example: "I'm looking for a job and Catherine suggested that you
    might have some advice for getting into the sales function of a
    large corporate" or "I'm thinking about changing career and
    moving into publishing, and Catherine suggested that you would
    be an excellent person to talk me through some of the pros and
    cons of working in publishing."

Over the page is an example of the basic structure of a networking
script.

"Hello. My name is _____ and I currently work as a _____. I got your name from _____ who knows you from _____. S/he suggested that I talk to you because I am currently _____. Would you have a few minutes to speak now or is there another, more convenient time when I could call you?"

If you're polite and professional enough, you may be surprised to find that most people will say "yes" to your request. So long as you are only asking for some of their time on the telephone, most people are only too pleased to help.

When deciding what you would like from the other person, remember that you are networking for two reasons:

1. To gather advice, information, and referrals from other people.
2. To raise your profile and remind people that you exist.

Take a look at the following examples of networking scripts:

- "Hello. My name's Marcus Carrick and I'm a human resources manager. Jeffrey Buckingham – who I believe used to be an ex-client of yours – suggested that I get in touch with you. Jeff said that you're really well connected with consumer goods companies so I was hoping to ask your advice as I'm currently looking to move into that sector. I'm not begging for a job – just looking for some advice. Would you have fifteen minutes at some time in the future when I could call you and hear some of your thoughts, please?"
- "Hi. My name's Alison Dale. I got your name from Laura Hollins, who suggested that you might be able to help. I'm thinking about changing career direction and becoming an acupuncturist. Laura suggested that you'd be a great person to talk to for advice as you did just that. Would you have fifteen or

twenty minutes to talk me through your experiences of it and 91
how you found the transition, please?"

So what are *you* going to say when you pick up the telephone?

Making your first call

When you've written your introductory script, you're ready to make your first call. Of course you want everyone in your network to be on the lookout for job vacancies and to recommend you for jobs. But before you can do that, you need to think about who to call first.

I recommend that you avoid calling the most influential and important people on your list first. To begin your networking campaign, practise on friends who won't mind if you mess up. Hone your networking skills and telephone manner on friends who may be less helpful, but with whom you have strong relationships.

Look over your prioritized list of contact names and choose a half-dozen people with whom you have "three tick" relationships that rate as only either "one star" or "two stars" in terms of potential usefulness. These "three tick" people – in other words, your friends – are more likely to forgive you if you are less than entirely smooth and professional. So it doesn't matter if you make a mistake.

Once you have worked through a few of your friends, ask yourself how those conversations went:

- Did you explain your situation and what you need clearly?
- Did you get the information and/or referrals to other people that you wanted?

Rookie Buster

To begin your networking campaign, practise on friends who won't mind if you mess up.

92   If you feel that you need further practice, keep calling friends until you have polished your telephone manner. Once you have built up your confidence, you can then work on people whom you rate more highly in terms of potential usefulness.

Making the most of networking conversations

Most people are more than happy to help. So what should you say to them once you get them back on the telephone (or even face to face)?

Whatever questions you decide to ask, bear in mind that preparation is the key here. You will need to prepare questions that suit your personal situation. But here are some suggestions.

Questions for career change

If you are looking to change careers, consider questions such as:

- What's the day-to-day work like? Could you talk me through an average week, please? What do you most enjoy and dislike?

- What are the typical working hours like?
- What are the financial rewards like to begin with? And how much do people tend to earn three, five, and ten years after they begin in it?

- How did you get into the field? What training or qualifications did you need? And do you know of any people who got into this field without that training or qualifications?

- As I'm thinking about entering this field, what advice would you have for me?

Questions about a specific organization 93

Sometimes you may be looking for help getting a job in a particular organization. Perhaps you have an interview coming up with the organization. Or you may just like the organization and want to work for it should any opportunities arise there.

Networking can allow you to gather more information about a specific organization. You may, for example, have tracked down someone who either currently works in that organization or previously worked there; or you may be speaking to someone who knows a lot about that company. Consider asking questions such as:

- What's the culture of the organization like?
- What are the pros and cons of working for the organization?
- Apart from what I've been able to find out in the general news and online, what else is there that you can tell me about the organization and the sector in which it competes?
- I have an interview there coming up – what advice can you offer me about the recruitment and selection process?

Rookie Buster

Networking can allow you to gather more information about a specific organization.

General questions for job hunters

As a smart job hunter, you should prepare questions for each and every person that you speak to. The questions you ask one person in your network are likely to be quite different from the ones you ask someone else. However, depending on the circumstances and how well you know someone, here are some more suggestions of questions that you could ask:

94

- I'd really like to work in your industry – if I send you my CV, could you give me a few minutes' worth of feedback please?
- I'm not asking you for a job, but if you come across any suitable opportunities, could you let me know, please?

Questions asking for further introductions

One of your aims whenever you speak to anyone should be to ask for introductions to further people. Remember that the purpose of networking is to *grow* the number of people who know you and could recommend you for a job. Consider asking for a referral every time you speak to someone new. Here are some suggestions for how you could phrase your requests:

- Can you think of anyone else I could speak to who might have information on the profession or advice on getting into it? And would you mind if I call them and mention your name?
- Can you think of anyone else I could speak to in order to get further information about the organization?
- I'd really like to work for your organization – can you think of anyone I could speak to, such as a human resources manager or a hiring manager that I could speak to?

Rookie Buster

Consider asking for a referral every time you speak to someone new.

Growing your network

Whenever possible, try to meet influential people (your "3-star" contacts in terms of usefulness) in person rather than speaking simply over the telephone. Ask for a mere 20 minutes of their time (because

20 minutes doesn't sound very much and so it makes it harder for people to turn it down). Offer to go to their workplace, to meet them for a coffee before work, a sandwich at lunch, or a drink after work.

Be sure to dress appropriately in work attire – even if you are currently not working. And be certain to behave in a professional and enthusiastic manner at all times. No matter how downtrodden you may feel about your job situation, treat such networking meetings as a possible interview. When networking, you are being evaluated as much for how you come across as for what you actually say. Even if the person you're speaking to doesn't have the power to offer you a job directly, he or she is still evaluating you and deciding whether to introduce you to other people who could possibly offer you a job.

Rookie Buster

When networking, you are being evaluated as much for how you come across as for what you actually say.

Maintaining your network

Speaking to people or meeting them once is only the start of the networking process. People are busy and – even if they have the best intentions of looking out for suitable job-leads for you – will tend to forget. It's up to you to maintain the relationship by reminding people that you exist.

Keeping track of your contacts

Be sure to write up notes after every phone call or meeting to summarize not only the work-related information that you wanted, but also the work and non-work information that people may share with you about themselves. Keep track of the fact that someone is moving house

96 or just got promoted, or that their daughter is taking an important set of exams in the next few months.

Doing so allows you to maintain a rapport. So if you get in touch again in the future, it allows you to drop these facts back into the conversation and make other people feel valued.

Looking for genuine reasons to get in touch

Look for mentions of a person's organization in the news and get back in touch if it seems appropriate. Forward articles or clippings that may be of interest. Sometimes you may wish to get in touch purely because something else you read or heard about has triggered a thought – for example "I met someone who does a very similar role to you but in a very different industry and it made me think of you. How are you?"

Get in touch and convey that other people are in your thoughts. Do it and they will be more likely to remember you and point you in the direction of job-leads.

Coach's notes

- Remember that networking simply involves picking up the telephone to ask friends and acquaintances for a few minutes of their time – there's nothing difficult or sinister about it!
- Refuse to network and you deprive yourself of a major asset when it comes to finding a job. Remember that between 50 and 85 per cent of all jobs are filled through word of mouth and networking!
- Kick off your networking campaign by listing *everyone* you know.
- Prepare a networking script to make sure that your conversations go smoothly.
- Hone your networking skill by practising first on sympathetic friends before you pursue the more influential (but possibly more challenging) people within your network.
- Always ask for introductions to further people, as that's the only way your network will grow!
- Keep notes on the people you encounter and think about ways to maintain the relationship with them so that they don't forget about you.

Go for it! Give networking a go and give yourself the best possible chance of securing a great job. A lot of people are too lazy to bother networking – but not you! Remember that networking is possibly the most powerful tool in your job-hunting kit. Start networking and you will almost certainly find that it is much easier (and more effective) than you might expect. No time like the present to give it a go!

Notes

Interviewers are looking to hire motivated and positive people. And when it comes to making up their minds, they are often less interested in *what* you say than *how* you say it. In this chapter, I talk you through how to use your tone of voice and body language to convince the interviewers that you're the perfect person for the job.

CHAPTER 6

Communicating with confidence

Understanding the importance of personal impact

When interviewers decide who to hire, the candidate with the best skills and experience does not always get the job! Many interviewers are heavily influenced in their decision-making by factors such as how candidates look and dress and speak, and whether they come across as likeable people. Interviewers are as interested in personal chemistry as they are in job competence. Many interviewers would rather hire someone they like, but who doesn't have quite the right skills, than someone who has the right skills, but comes across as boring or arrogant!

If you want to get the job, you must manage your personal impact – how you come across. You must present yourself as the person who you think the employer is looking for. Think of an interview as a first date. If you go on a date with someone you're attracted to, I'll bet that you probably make a bit more of an effort than usual.

So in your next interview, if you know that you can be a little shy, then try to be more gregarious. If you know that you are a bit loud,

102 then try to quieten down. Behave in the way that the employer would like to see, and you're more likely to get offered the job. You could always turn the job down – but at least then you have the luxury of choosing whether to turn the job down or not, rather than having the employer reject you for "being yourself".

Rookie Buster

Behave in the way that the employer would like to see, and you're more likely to get offered the job.

Dressing to impress

We all make snap judgements about each other. See a man wearing black leather trousers, black eye make-up and multiple piercings in his face, and you may get a certain instant impression of him. See a woman with greasy hair wearing stained trousers and a dirty t-shirt and you may make another judgement.

You can help to ensure that the interviewers think you are suitable for the job by paying attention to how you dress and look. But wearing a suit may not always be your best option. For example, if you're going for a job working in a "creative" industry such as advertising or fashion, the people there may see people who wear suits as stuffy and dull! Instead follow these steps to decide how best to dress:

1. Telephone the switchboard of the organization and ask about the dress code. Explain that you have an interview and want to check what to wear so that you do not commit a sartorial mistake. If you can, avoid being fobbed off by a receptionist. Try to speak to the secretary or assistant of the manager who will be interviewing you.

2. Visit the office of your chosen employer and stand outside the
   building for a few minutes. Observe the people walking through
   reception and take note of what they are wearing. If most people
   are in smart suits or casual clothes or highly fashionable clothes,
   you should try to dress accordingly.

If in doubt, wear a suit. You're better off dressing a little too smartly
than being underdressed. For example, a man who is wearing a suit
and tie can simply take off his tie and unbutton his top button to appear
less formal; women should look for a skirt and top combination that
would be appropriate in either fairly formal or more relaxed
circumstances.

Rookie Buster

You're better off dressing a little too smartly than being
underdressed.

Conveying confidence through body language

Employers want to hire people who are at least reasonably confident.
So have a think about what that means for the different aspects of your
body language.

Maintaining eye contact

Think about people you may know who constantly avoid eye contact.
They may come across as shy or guilty – or both! So you will win points
with an interviewer for making strong eye contact.

As a rule of thumb, try to look at the interviewers in the eyes (for at
least 90 per cent of the time) when they are speaking or asking you

104   questions. And when you are answering an interview question, aim to maintain eye contact for at least 60 to 70 per cent of the time. However, feel free to look away occasionally – for example, many people look away into the middle distance when thinking about the right way to answer an interview question.

Demonstrating "active listening"

Just paying attention to the interviewer isn't good enough; the interviewer must *actively see* that you are paying attention. Good candidates use a technique called "active listening" to demonstrate visibly to an interviewer that they are listening to the interviewer's every word.

In order to use this technique, aim to:

- Nod occasionally when the interviewer speaks, to show that you understand what is being said.
- "Flash" your eyes occasionally by raising your eyebrows. Again, this shows that you are paying attention to the interviewer's words.
- Use vocal cues such as "uh-huh", "yes" and "mm-hmm" intermittently to give the interviewer confirmation that you are following the gist of the conversation.

Rookie Buster

Just paying attention to the interviewer isn't good enough; the interviewer must *actively see* that you are paying attention.

If you're not sure how "active listening" works in practice, then watch your friends or colleagues when you next meet them. You'll see how they use their head movements, facial expressions and verbal utterances to show they're listening to you.

Using your hands and body   105

Your posture and use of physical movement send out clear signals about how you may feel during the interview. To ensure that you project an aura of confidence (even if you may not feel it!) be sure to:

- **Keep your posture upright at all times**. Imagine that there's a piece of string attached to the top of your head and that someone is pulling it towards the ceiling. Avoid letting your shoulders hunch forwards if you're perhaps nervous or tired.
- **Avoid fidgeting**. People who play with or even keep touching their jewellery, hair or keys come across as restless and lacking in confidence. Keep your hands still and visible – perhaps on the armrests of your chair, clasped lightly in your lap or in front of you on the table if there is one.
- **Use your hands to emphasize key points**. Research shows that candidates who use hand gestures come across as more sincere and credible. So use your hands occasionally to make yourself more visually engaging – for example by counting points off on your fingers or moving your hands to illustrate the stories you tell.
- **Avoid crossing your arms or legs**. Some interviewers believe that crossing your arms or even your legs is a sign of defensiveness. So don't do either.
- **Keep any movement slow and fluid**. Whether you are shifting posture, moving your feet to get more comfortable, or making gestures with your hands, avoid making rapid, jagged movements, as these can convey nervousness. Make any movements slow and almost unnoticeable so that the interviewer can pay attention to what you say rather than your physical movements or twitches!

Speaking with confidence

Interviewers frequently complain about being forced to listen to monotonous candidates droning on and on about their experiences. So be sure to enliven your interview responses through tone of voice and inflection:

106

- **Consider the loudness of your voice**. Have you ever been told that you speak a bit too quietly or loudly? Being barely audible will make you sound like a shy, weak candidate; being too loud could make you seem bossy and arrogant.
- **Vary the tone and pace of your voice**. If you're speaking about an achievement or something that you should be excited about, be sure to speak in an enthusiastic (in other words, slightly higher pitched and moderately quicker) tone of voice. If you're being asked to talk about difficult circumstances, problems or serious issues, you should speak in a more sombre tone (that is, by deepening your voice and speaking more slowly).
- **Articulate your words with care**. Nervous candidates often mumble their words. So make sure that you pronounce your words carefully.

If you're at all prone to nervousness, run through a mock interview with a friend and ask for candid feedback on how you sound. Even better if you can record your voice or even videotape your entire performance to see and hear how you look and sound.

Projecting a positive and upbeat demeanour

The job market can be quite a rollercoaster. People sometimes get fired or get into nasty disagreements with their previous employers. Plus more and more people are finding themselves being made redundant – often through no fault of their own. If that has happened to you, I can understand that you may be feeling glum or sad, slightly resentful or downright angry.

However, interviewers only want to hire positive, upbeat people! So
if you feel any negative emotions, you need to hold them in check to
maximize your chances of getting offered a job.

If you feel that you have suffered some terrible injustice, try the following expressive writing exercise to help you to let go of the past and
prepare for a brighter future. You will need 30 minutes away from dis-
tractions. Take a sheet of paper and:

1. Spend 10 to 15 minutes simply writing (or typing) about how you
   feel. You must write about not only about the unfortunate
   experience(s) but also the emotions that you feel as a result of
   them.
2. Then spend another 10 to 15 minutes writing about your hopes
   and goals in your life and work. What are you realistically hoping
   to achieve, both in your career and outside your work?

In your writing, make sure you explore your deepest emotions and
thoughts. No one else will ever see what you write – this exercise is
solely for your benefit. Don't worry about spelling or grammar. Just be
totally honest about what you are thinking and feeling, your worries
and fears, hopes and dreams. The only rule is that you keep writing for
the full 30 minutes.

Once you have finished, take what you've written and seal it away
in an envelope, symbolically distancing yourself from the past and the
emotions that go along with it.

Now, you may wonder about the point of this exercise. But trust
me: I'm a trained psychologist. In fact, a research study showed that
this technique helped a group of job hunters to find new jobs more
quickly than job hunters who did not use the technique. For whatever
reason, this technique works. Use it!

Handling pre-interview nerves

Many people are their own worst enemies when it comes to interviews. If
you ever feel nervous before interviews, you may find thoughts running
through your head such as "I'll never get the job" or "I'm terrible at

interviews". And then, during the interview, you probably over-think everything you say, with the little voice inside your head making comments such as "No – that was such a stupid answer!" or "The interviewer looks bored – I must be a bad candidate!"

Psychologists call such thoughts *automatic negative thoughts*, or ANTs for short. These ANTs seem to pop unbidden into your consciousness and can be very damaging to your confidence. But the good news is that you can make a conscious effort to combat them.

Using your personal confidence coach

You can put a stop to the inner voice coming out with negative comments such as "this won't turn out well" or "I hate interviews". Psychologists have found that you can drown out the ANTs by preparing a set of positive statements about yourself. I call these positive statements *capability-affirming thoughts*, or CATs.

Many people hire personal trainers to help them exercise. A personal trainer might say something like "Come on – just two more minutes on the treadmill!" or "Only three more press-ups to go – you've done so well, you're fantastic!" Now imagine a personal coach whom you have hired to help to boost your confidence – what would your coach say to you? Here are examples of the kind of positive comments that a confidence coach might shout at you to urge you on:

- "Stay confident – you can do it!"
- "You can stay positive if you want to."
- "Keep smiling."
- "You've got great skills and the right experience – you'll get this job!"
- "Come on, you've survived interviews before and you can do it again!"

Now take a few minutes to write down a handful of positive statements that you think would help to spur *you* on. Jot these CATs on a sheet of paper or a small piece of card to keep at hand.

Whenever you need a lift – whether that's when you're feeling

despondent sat at home writing CVs and covering letters or in the
moments just before you go into an interview – repeat these CATs
under your breath to yourself. Imagine that someone – your personal
coach – is shouting these to you from just over your shoulder. Keep
doing it and you can banish those worrisome thoughts from your
head.

This works. Do it.

Rookie Buster

Imagine a personal coach whom you have hired to help
to boost your confidence – what would your coach say to
you?

Counting down to your interview

Job hunters sometimes let themselves down because they don't get
their preparations right just before the interview. A little advance planning will help you to stride into your interview full of confidence.
Make sure you work through these positive steps:

1. **Familiarize yourself with the time, date and location for your
   interview**. Make sure you check where and when you are
   supposed to turn up for your interview. I have personally had
   more than one candidate who has turned up a week too early
   because they misread the date on their letters!
2. **Plan your journey to the interview**. If you are not sure about
   how to get to your interview, be certain to plan your route and
   journey time so that you can turn up with time to spare.
3. **Get your outfit ready the night before**. Nothing worse than
   getting ready to set off for your interview only to find that your
   favourite item of clothing is creased or has a stain on it.
4. **Print out copies of your CV to take along**. Interviewers
   sometimes misplace CVs just prior to an interview. So be ready to

110   hand pristine copies of your CV to the interviewer(s) if they don't have it to hand.

5. **Take a quality newspaper with you that morning**. If you arrive at the location of the interview more than 30 minutes early, go find a café and read the newspaper, as some interviewers interpret being too early as over-anxiousness.

Rookie Buster

A little advance planning will help you to stride into your interview full of confidence.

Making your first impression count

Be aware that most interviewers (and in fact most people) are unduly swayed by first impressions. You can create a really positive and lasting impact by making a concerted effort during those first few minutes. So be sure to make a great first impression by following these pointers:

1. **Pre-plan fragments of small talk**. Arrive at reception at least 10 or 15 minutes early and look around you for features that you could genuinely praise. So when the interviewer arrives, you can make some complimentary comment such as "I really love the artwork you have on the walls here," "Your receptionist is really friendly!" or "You're lucky to have such a lot of light coming through into your reception." So long as your comment is genuine, you will come across immediately as positive and interesting.

2. **Watch out for smells and stickiness!** Pop a sugar-free breath mint into your mouth while you wait in reception. And just as you

see the interviewer approach you, discreetly wipe your right hand
either on a handkerchief in your pocket or even on the back of
your trouser leg or skirt. You want a dry palm – not a sweaty one
– before shaking hands.

3. **Smile warmly and offer a strong handshake as you introduce
   yourself**. Smile broadly and extend your hand. Make sure you
   grasp the interviewer's hand reasonably firmly – as there's nothing
   worse than a "limp squid" handshake. Pump the interviewer's
   hand at most three times. "I'm Jack Horsley – pleased to meet
   you."

4. **Follow the interviewer's lead with respect to small talk**. Engage
   in polite conversation if the interviewer seems amenable to it. If
   the interviewer is talkative, be prepared to talk about your
   journey, the weather, the organization's offices, and other
   innocuous topics. If the interviewer is quieter, you should be more
   reticent too. Whatever you talk about, try to be positive – or at
   least neutral rather than negative – even if your journey was
   terrible, the weather is lousy and the receptionist was rude!

Rookie Buster

Be aware that most interviewers (and in fact most
people) are unduly swayed by first impressions.

Coach's notes

- Never forget that interviewers are often as interested in how you come across as in the skills and experience you have. Make a real effort to project a positive attitude at all times.
- Consider how you can choreograph the different aspects of your body language (for example, eye contact, "active listening" cues, and hand and body movements) to create a calm, confident demeanour.
- Think also about the qualities of your voice – be sure to match them to the needs of your particular interview situation.
- Be especially careful if you hold any negative feelings such as sadness or anger about your current or previous employers. Use the expressive writing technique to free yourself of any psychological baggage.
- Imagine that you have a personal confidence coach whispering positive comments into your head. What would yours say to you?
- Plan the 24 hours prior to your interview to ensure that you can arrive in a collected frame of mind rather than feeling frantic because you have had to rush.
- Remember that first impressions really *do* count. So make sure that yours counts in the right way.

Go for it! Remember that confidence isn't a quality that you're either born with or born without. You can develop greater levels of confidence if you put your mind to it. Think about the different aspects of your body language. Project an aura of confidence. And use the psychological techniques in this chapter to chase away those worries and doubts. Trust me – I'm a psychologist – you *can* feel more confident.

114 **Notes**

Notes

It's time to think about what you're going to say during the interview. The good news is that you don't have to memorize answers to 101 different interview questions. All you need to do is prepare a handful of stories and be ready to deliver them in a way that showcases how you have used your skills and qualities to deliver results.

CHAPTER 7

Impressing interviewers with your competence and capability

Talking about essential interview themes

Interviewers can ask many questions, but thankfully you don't have to memorize answers to every single question. All you need to do is prepare to answer questions covering the following four themes:

1. **Questions about your capability** – in other words, "What can you do for us?" Interviewers are probably most focused on how you can use your skills and knowledge to help them achieve organizational goals.

2. **Questions about chemistry** – in other words, "Will we like you and get along with you?" Employers don't just want to hire talented people; they also want to hire friendly people with similar values to the rest of the team.

3. **Questions about your commitment** – in other words, "Why do you want to work for this organization?" Employers prefer to hire people who want to work for their particular organization rather than people who would be content with just a job.

4. **Questions about cash** – in other words, "How much will it cost us to hire you?" In many situations, the pay package may not be up for negotiation; however, in some cases an employer may be willing to pay more in order to hire exceptional candidates.

Let's cover how to respond to questions about these four categories of questions in the rest of this chapter and in Chapter 8.

Understanding the golden rules when talking about your capability

Most of an interviewer's questions will focus on your capability – that is, your ability to do the job and deliver results. If you follow these six rules, you will go a long way to making a strong impression.

Rule 1: Explain problems solved and results achieved

Interviewers are not terribly interested in hiring people who have worked hard or merely kept busy in their previous jobs. So spending lots of time telling an interviewer about your day-to-day work or responsibilities will have little impact on them.

Interviewers want to hire people who can solve problems and deliver results for them. So be sure to spend most of your time sharing stories about problems you have solved and results you have delivered for your current or previous employers.

Rookie Buster

Interviewers want to hire people who can solve problems and deliver results for them.

Rule 2: Provide evidence for your assertions   119

Many interviewers are trained to listen for evidence of how you have put your skills into use. Avoid giving only personal opinions about yourself and instead tell interviewers the evidence that you have for your beliefs. Whenever possible, use any positive feedback or comments (whether verbal or written) that you received to back up your claims.

Compare the following examples:

Assertion without evidence = unimpressive
- "I believe the customer was happy with her purchase."
- "I am an exceptional sales person."

Assertion with evidence = impressive
- "The customer told me how happy she was with her purchase."
- "In my last evaluation, my boss wrote a comment saying that I was one of the strongest sales people she had ever had in her team."

If you have actual examples or evidence that you can bring along, then use that as well. Bring along a portfolio of your work, including:
- Samples of your work, such as drawings, diagrams, items of clothing you have made, photographs you have taken, or whatever might be appropriate for your field of work.
- Proofs of performance including awards, testimonials, positive evaluations or appraisals, letters of commendation, and so on.

Rookie Buster

Avoid giving only personal opinions about yourself and instead tell interviewers the evidence that you have for your beliefs.

120   Never present items from your portfolio without permission. But do mention them if appropriate to strengthen your case. For example, rather than simply saying "In my last evaluation, my boss wrote a comment saying that I was one of the strongest sales people she had ever had in her team," you could say: "In my last evaluation, my boss wrote a comment saying that I was one of the strongest sales people she had ever had in her team. I've got a copy of the evaluation here if you'd like to see it."

Rule 3: KISS your answers

Interviewers hate candidates who drone on and on. So "Keep It Short and Sweet" (KISS). Whenever you answer a question, aim to keep your response to less than two minutes. If you haven't finished your story within that time, at least check that what you're saying is useful by asking the interviewer a question such as:
- "Is this the kind of response you were looking for?"
- "Shall I go on?"

By asking such a question, you give interviewers the opportunity to steer you in the right direction or ask you an entirely different question if what you're saying is not what they were looking for.

Rookie Buster

Whenever you answer a question, aim to keep your response to less than two minutes.

Rule 4: Answer the question that was actually asked

One of the dangers of memorizing answers to questions in advance is that some candidates end up regurgitating a response regardless of the question that was actually asked! So make sure you listen carefully to the question and answer it – rather than answering the question you would *like* to answer.

If you are in any way uncertain about the question – for example if an interviewer uses terminology you aren't familiar with or if the interviewer asks a lengthy question with many parts to it – *do* ask the interviewer to rephrase the question:

- "Sorry – I didn't catch all of that, could you repeat that last bit for me again, please?"
- "I'd love to answer the question, but I'm not familiar with the term 'TQM'. Could you explain what you mean by that, please?"

Rule 5: Meet the employer's needs – not yours

Some candidates fall into the trap of going into an interview and talking about what they want. They ask questions like "How much do you pay?" or "How much time off will I get?" Unfortunately, interviewers *hate* candidates who seem to be most interested in what they can expect from the employer.

Interviewers want to hire candidates who are more interested in how they can help the employer to meet its goals. Remember at all times that your attitude must be "How can I help this organization to succeed?" rather than "What can I get out of this organization?"

Rookie Buster

Remember at all times that your attitude must be "How can I help this organization to succeed?" rather than "What can I get out of this organization?"

122 ## Rule 6: Match your manner to the topics you discuss

I have already mentioned in Chapter 6 that *how* you speak can make as much of an impact as *what* you say. Candidates who relay facts and stories in a calm and emotionless manner don't always win over interviewers. The most successful candidates are those who can relay facts and stories in a positive, enthusiastic way.

Think of yourself as an actor – albeit on a chair instead of a stage, and playing to a very small audience of only a few interviewers. Actors who recite their lines without emotion are dull and don't seem believable. Great actors always use their feelings to grab the attention of their audience. And that's what you need to do too.

So make sure you appear pleased and happy when talking about your past achievements. Get across your enthusiasm when answering questions about why you want to work for this organization. Speak in a more sober fashion if you need to talk about unfortunate circumstances or difficult times.

Rookie Buster

The most successful candidates are those who can relay facts and stories in a positive, enthusiastic way.

Constructing answers to questions about your capability

I've mentioned several times (in previous chapters as well as in this one) that employers are most interested in candidates who can demonstrate how they have used their skills to deliver results on behalf of their employers.

Showing the interviewers your CAR   123

To create success stories with which to impress interviewers about how you have delivered such results, you should use the acronym CAR:

- **C – Challenge** – what was the situation? Aim to explain in just a couple of sentences the problem or issue that you had to tackle. Bear in mind that you should spend as little time as possible talking about the background so that you can focus on the next part, the actions.
- **A – Actions** – what specific actions did you take in order to deal with the problem or situation? Interviewers are most interested in the actions you took – so spend most of your time talking through your actions.
- **R – Result(s)** – what was the outcome (hopefully a positive one) that you got as a consequence of your actions? And, if you had to do it again, what did you learn from the results you attained?

Using a worksheet to capture your success stories

Use the worksheet on the next page to prepare success stories to tell interviewers. Work through the five questions to arm yourself so that you can give interviewers as much (or as little) information and detail as they need. For example, some interviewers may not ask questions 2 ("Who else was involved or affected?") or 5 ("What did you learn?"). However, working through the worksheet in a methodical way will help you to prepare for just about any interview situation.

124

Challenge

Q1. What was the situation?

Q2. Who else was involved or affected?

Actions

Q3. What steps or decisions did you take?

Step 1:

Step 2:

Step 3:

Step 4:

Etc. (continue to write other actions on a blank sheet if necessary)

Results

Q4. What was the eventual outcome? (Ideally, quantify with numbers)

Q5. What did you learn?

Have a look back at the section "Matching what you have with what   125
the employer wants" (on page 46). Look again at the list of skills and
knowledge that the employer needs. And then complete the worksheet
twice for every skill. You need to have two stories for every skill that
the employer wants. Either photocopy the worksheet or simply write
out the answers to the questions on blank sheets of paper.

Rookie Buster

You need to have two stories for every skill that the
employer wants.

Example: completed worksheet

There's an example of a completed worksheet on page 126. The candidate has identified that the organization needs someone with planning
and organization skills.

Once you have completed the worksheet to cover all of the skills
that the employer needs for this role, you can use it in response to
many questions. The completed worksheet could be used to answer a
range of questions including:

- "Tell me about a project that you're proud of."
- "What are your major achievements?"
- "We need people who are good at planning and organizing – do
  you have much experience of that?"

Please do take the time to complete your own worksheet. Once you
have completed it *twice* for every skill that the employer needs for this
role, you can be sure that you will be able to answer just about any
question about your capability that an interviewer could throw at you.

Challenge

Q1. What was the situation? *My boss (Diana) asked me to plan the annual summer party. She gave me a budget of £4,000 for the entire department, which was 10 per cent less than what her previous assistant had to organize the previous year's party.*

Q2. Who else was involved or affected? *120 staff in our department; suppliers such as hotel venues and caterers.*

Actions

Q3. What steps or decisions did you take?

Step 1: *When Diana asked me to plan the party, I sent out an email to the entire department asking what they liked and didn't like about last year's party.*

Step 2: *I reviewed the comments and discovered that people said the food hadn't been very good and that the venue didn't have enough car parking.*

Step 3: *I contacted 8 venues to decide on the right location (one with enough parking). Also contacted 6 caterers to discuss menus within my budget.*

Step 4: *I wrote a business case laying out the options and presented them to Diana; she agreed that my favoured venue and caterer were also ones she liked.*

Etc. (continue to write other actions on a blank sheet if necessary)

Results

Q4. What was the eventual outcome? (Ideally, quantify with numbers) *Party was a great success – we had 107 people turn up (compared with only 90-something the previous year). And great comments in person and by email from satisfied colleagues.*

Q5. What did you learn? *You can get a good deal with suppliers if you negotiate well with them and play them off against each other. Also the importance of getting feedback from stakeholders (i.e. colleagues in department).*

Coach's notes

- Remember to tell interviewers about problems you have solved and results you have achieved rather than merely your day-to-day duties and responsibilities.
- Quantify your interview answers whenever possible and aim to speak for no more than two minutes at a time if you can.
- Rather than memorize answers to 101 questions, prepare instead to answer questions on just four topics: your capability ("What can you do for us?"), the interpersonal chemistry ("Will we like you and get along with you?"), your commitment ("Why do you want to work for this organization?") and cash ("How much will it cost us to hire you?"). I cover chemistry, commitment and cash in the next chapter.
- In answering questions to showcase your skills and achievements, use the CAR acronym to explain the Challenge, Actions you took, and Results you attained.
- Complete the interview story worksheet *twice* for every skill that the employer requires for success in the role.

Go for it! Stand out from the crowd by doing some interview prep. Focus on just four basic topics and you can be certain you'll make a great impact during an interview. Simply consider the skills that the employer needs and then list all of the occasions in which you have put those skills into action. That's all you need to do. Go on, do it now!

Notes

Constructing interview answers to talk about your capability and skills will help you to go a long way. But this chapter will equip you with the means to answer questions about chemistry with the rest of the team, your commitment, your cash and salary requirements, and even any concerns that interviewers may have. Read this chapter if you want to have the interviewers begging to give you a job!

CHAPTER 8

Chemistry, commitment and cash: handling interviewers' concerns

Answering questions about chemistry during the interview

Interviewers want to figure out whether you will get on with the rest of the team. In order to convince interviewers that you are a likeable person who will quickly build new relationships and become an asset to the rest of the team, you need bear in mind only three key principles:

1. **Be positive.** For example, focus on what was good about your boss, colleagues and organization rather than dwell on what was wrong with them. Even if you didn't get on with your last boss and are asked "What was your boss's biggest fault?", be sure to be positive. If you need to talk about the reasons you are leaving an organization, phrase your response in terms of what the new job will offer you rather than why you need to get away. Never speak ill of your current or previous colleagues, as it will only backfire and make you look like a whiner and bad-mouther.

2. **Give short examples to back up your assertions.** As with questions about your capability, anyone can make hollow claims.

132   Would you necessarily believe someone who says "I get on well with everyone, as I know everyone loves me and they'd hate to lose me"? Perhaps not. But I know that I'd be more likely to believe candidates who can give reasons why they think they are popular, such as "I get on well with everyone – for example, I'm as likely to get invited out for lunch by our managing director as some of the junior assistants."

3. **Tell the interviewers the answer that you think they want to hear**. When answering questions about your values or how much you socialize, bear in mind that different organizations may have different norms. For example, a small, entrepreneurial firm with an average age of 25 may place a lot more emphasis on having fun and socializing with each other; a large organization with many tens of thousands of staff and a much more conservative approach to business may take a dim view of too much socializing. So be careful to tailor your interview responses to what you think the interviewers are expecting to hear.

Rookie Buster

Never speak ill of your current or previous colleagues, as it will only backfire and make you look like a whiner and bad-mouther.

Matching your manner with your words

Remember that chemistry is established not only by *what* you say but also *how* you say it (have a look back at Chapter 6). So, above all, you must allow your positive nature and enthusiasm to come to the surface when answering questions about how you deal with colleagues – both the ones you get on with as well as the difficult people in the team.

Demonstrating your commitment during the interview

Interviewers are on the lookout for candidates who want to work for their particular organization. After all, if you were looking to hire someone, wouldn't you rather take on someone who desperately wants to work for you rather than someone who is simply looking for a job to pay the bills?

Putting across your dedication

Demonstrating your commitment through your interview answers is very simple to do. Simply follow these three rules:

1. **Do your research on the organization**. Be sure to read the organization's website and any brochures or marketing literature. Do some online searches to find out about the organization, its competitors and the sector or industry in general. Have a look back to the section "Researching employers" in Chapter 2 for a reminder on how to research effectively.

2. **Demonstrate your research by mentioning what you know about the organization in your interview answers**. All the research in the world is of no use unless you can *mention* pertinent facts in your interview responses.

3. **Make sure that you get across your passion and enthusiasm for working for the organization**. Focus on the positive aspects of the organization or the work that draw you to the vacancy at this particular organization.

Rookie Buster

All the research in the world is of no use unless you can *mention* pertinent facts in your interview responses.

134 Understanding how to answer specific questions on your level of commitment

Here are some of the commonest questions asked by interviewers and some advice on how to answer them:

Question: "Why do you want to work for us?"

Advice: Choose two or three key features of this organization or the role and repeat them back to the interviewers. For example, if the organization prides itself on its training programme or the awards it has won, then mention them as part of your response.

Question: "What do you know about our business?"

Advice: Rather than repeat back everything you know about the organization, try to highlight a current issue facing it that you could help with. For example, perhaps the company is trying to expand and you have experience of having helped a previous organization to grow in size.

Question: "Where do you see yourself in five years' time?"

Advice: Aim to discover in your research the likely career path for people who join the organization. You should then ideally be able to answer this question by saying that you would like to learn, grow and progress within the organization.

Question: "How would you compare us to our competitors?"

Advice: Look in your research for some way to compare this employer favourably with its competitors. Of course the interviewer believes that his or her organization is special – so you must respond by telling the interviewers why you believe this organization is better too.

Question: "How would you describe your ideal job?"   135
Advice: Avoid talking about what you might like to be doing (pop star, beauty contest judge, TV presenter, etc.). Instead, tell the interviewers that the role on offer with this organization fits many of your needs (for career development, stability, excitement, interesting work or whatever else you think is appropriate).

Handling questions about cash

Everyone works to earn a living. But one of the unspoken rules of interviewing is that you should never bring the topic of money up.

Understanding the reasons not to talk about cash

Here are three reasons you should avoid bringing up money:

1. If you ask about the money too early on, you risk sounding like a candidate who is greedy and only interested in how much the job can pay. Interviewers prefer to hire candidates who are more interested in the intrinsic nature of the job, opportunities for career development, the brand of the organization and so on.
2. You risk pricing yourself out of the market. Mention your salary during the early stages of the interviewing process and the interviewers could decide to cut short the interview. In contrast, by waiting until you have won over the interviewers, you stand a better chance of having the interviewers reconsider how much they might be willing to pay for the right candidate (you!).
3. You may compromise your ability to negotiate a deal if you mention too low a figure. By waiting for the employer to mention how much the organization is willing to pay first, you gain an advantage in deciding how much to ask for.

136

Rookie Buster

If you ask about the money too early on, you risk sounding like a candidate who is greedy and only interested in how much the job can pay.

Deflecting questions about cash

Your best option is to avoid discussing the issue of money at all. Talk about money only if the interviewer brings it up first. To get the job, aim to convince the interviewers that you are interested in the challenge of the job rather than just a big pay cheque.

If asked questions about money such as "How much do you earn?" or "How much will we need to pay you?", try to deflect the questions. Consider the following examples:

- "What I hope to do is convince you that my salary requirements are not the main issue here. I'm more interested in finding the right opportunity to develop my skills within an organization that has a strong brand. If we can do that, then I'm sure we can both be flexible on salary."
- "How much I earn isn't the issue here. I've read so much about your proposed new products that I'm really keen to get involved. I think that my track record of having helped to launch new products in my current role would make me a real asset to the team."

Rookie Buster

Talk about money only if the interviewer brings it up first.

However, if the interviewer persists and asks a more pointed question about money, you may have to give a response. When forced to talk about money, try to give a *range* rather than a specific figure. And then go on to restate the fact that you are interested in this organization or role for particular, positive reasons. Consider:

- "I'm after something in the region of £22,000 to £25,000, but as I said earlier, the precise salary is less important than finding a job that will both challenge and develop me as a manager."
- "I currently have a salary and bonus of around £33,000. However, I am more interested in securing a role such as this one that will give me direct client contact, which will allow me to progress towards my goal of moving into general management."

Rookie Buster

When forced to talk about money, try to give a *range* rather than a specific figure.

Fending off interviewers' concerns

Many candidates have an area of weakness that they'd rather not talk about. Such issues include (but are not limited to):

- Having a gap in your employment record.
- Being deficient in terms of a particular skill.
- A history of poor health.
- The lack of a critical qualification.
- Being overqualified or too experienced for the job.
- Having left a previous employer under compromising circumstances, such as being fired or having clashed with a previous boss.

Most candidates simply *hope* that the topic won't come up during the interview. But hoping isn't a strategy! And worrying that the topic might crop up is not going to help you to radiate confidence.

138   If you have an area of weakness, you should prepare a positioning statement to put it in the best possible light. Work out the precise words that you would use to put a positive spin on your particular issue(s). Consider the following examples:

- "I realize that I don't have a degree, but I recall from your advert that you said that a degree would be desirable rather than a requirement. Instead, what I do possess is..." (and then the candidate goes on to talk about a strength that that is much more positive instead).

- "Yes, there is a gap of 11 months between having left Impresario Interim Consulting and my current role. I suffered a physical illness brought on by an infection, which meant that I was unable to work. However, my doctors have assured me that I am entirely recovered. During a particularly busy period a few months ago when our head office systems suffered from severe problems, I was able to work 50 to 60 hours a week for several weeks to clear a backlog of customer orders. And, as you can see, I have a strong track record of..." (and, again, the candidate goes on to talk about various positive selling points instead).

Rookie Buster

If you have an area of weakness, you should prepare a positioning statement to put it in the best possible light.

Then, if the interviewer should ask about your area of weakness, you can recite your carefully worded answer. Your aim should be to deflect the interviewer's concerns by answering the question briefly and positively and then moving on to an entirely different, more positive topic.

Coach's notes

- Remember that chemistry is key when it comes to finding a job. Aim to be unfailingly positive when speaking about your relationships with current or previous bosses and colleagues.
- Weave your knowledge and insights about the organization into your interview answers to convince interviewers that you are committed to securing a job with this particular organization more than any other.
- Avoid bringing up the topic of cash unless the interviewer brings it up. Even then, try to deflect such questions by talking about other reasons why you want the job.
- Prepare positioning statements in the event that an interviewer should ask you about an area of weakness. Preparing to put a positive spin on your situation is a better tactic than hoping the interviewer won't ask you about it!

Go for it! There's a saying that the best-prepared candidate (rather than the best candidate) usually gets the job. Give yourself a pat on the back because *you* are now the best-prepared candidate. Follow the advice in this chapter and you will be fully equipped to answer questions on your capability, your chemistry with the rest of the team, your commitments, cash requirements and any interviewers' concerns. Get ready to land that job!

Notes

Interviewers are a fundamentally lazy breed. Rather than come up with different questions to challenge and cross-examine candidates, they usually rely on recycling the same questions again and again. But that's good news for you. In this chapter I talk you through how to craft sterling answers to the six most frequently asked interview questions.

CHAPTER 9

Preparing top answers to the "super six" questions

"Tell us about yourself"

Some interviewers like to begin interviews with this question. The open-ended nature of the question means that you could potentially answer it in many different ways, such as by talking about your personal or family life or your work.

However, remember that your sole objective during the interview is to persuade the interviewer that you possess the ability to deliver results for the organization. So use this question as an opportunity to focus immediately on your top qualities. Answer this question as if an interviewer had asked you: "Tell us about your recent career, focusing on the two or three key reasons we should hire you."

Rookie Buster

Remember that your sole objective during the interview is to persuade the interviewer that you possess the ability to deliver results for the organization.

144 Remember to tailor your responses based not only on your own experience but also on the needs of the particular employer. Use the following examples of responses to inspire your own answer:

- "I have been working as an account manager for five years and am now looking to progress by taking on a larger team in a more dynamic environment such as yours. I think that three things stand out on my CV. Firstly, that I have a track record of delivering and exceeding targets: I exceeded my sales targets in three out of the last four years and I have always been in the top 20 per cent of our account management team in terms of performance. Secondly, I have strong coaching skills, having coached and developed three of my team from fairly junior roles into assuming account management responsibilities of their own. Thirdly, I was ranked among the top 25 per cent of managers in terms of performance across the department of 14 managers."
- "I am a teacher with a passion for growing the confidence of the students that I teach. When I came into my current job, our school was struggling quite badly and performing in the bottom quartile of the regional league tables in terms of standardized test performance. But I've been part of the team that has helped to push our results up for the last three years in a row. I can tell you in more detail about some of the initiatives I've either been involved in or led, but these include: a series of after-school workshops for students who wanted coaching on handling exam nerves; a project to revamp the timetable to put a greater focus on basic arithmetic where we had the greatest performance gaps; and an initiative to get parents more involved in helping their children with homework and attendance. Is there any particular aspect of my career that you'd like to focus on?"

Other ways to begin your own answer include:
- "My background is unique because..."
- "Throughout my career, I have demonstrated that I..."
- "I have developed a reputation for..."
- "Clients frequently say that I..."

By preparing for this question, you will also be ready to tackle   145
similar questions such as:
- "Talk us through your career."
- "Could you start by telling us what makes you right for this role?"

"Why do you want to work for us?"

Remember that employers want to hire people who want to work for them, rather than people who are just on the lookout for a job with the first employer who will offer them one. In constructing your answer, be sure to demonstrate some insights from the research you have conducted on the industry and this particular organization. And remember to be positive; focus on why you want to work for this organization rather than why you may need to leave a bad situation.

Consider these sample answers:
- "The next step in my career is to work on much larger projects. And I'm particularly drawn to you because of the more rapid growth that your firm has achieved in the last two or three years. From my understanding of the marketplace, it seems that mid-sized firms such as yours are uniquely positioned to continue to grow. But apart from your growth rate, I have to say that yours was the only recruitment brochure that seemed to have a sense of humour. Many of your competitors focused only on what made them great to work for. But yours seemed to focus equally both on why you're great for a person's career and also on the team ethos and enjoying the work that you do."
- "A couple of things stand out. Yours is the only pharmaceutical business that has consistently invested at least 15 per cent of your net profits into research and development. I see that as a major competitive advantage, given that most pharma businesses are relying on older drugs and don't seem to have many new ones in development. I am also drawn to your business because of the CEO's ambition to make environmental sustainability a key plank of the business in the coming years."

Rookie Buster

Remember to be positive; focus on why you want to work for this organization rather than why you may need to leave a bad situation.

In responding to this question, think about other features or benefits that you could praise about a particular employer, such as:

- Its size (for example, smaller firms may have more of a family feel, while larger firms may have better-established training and development programmes).
- Its reputation in the marketplace.
- Awards it has won.
- New products or services that make it stand out from its competitors.
- Its ambitions or goals.
- Opportunities to travel and/or work abroad.

So why do *you* want to work for any particular organization?

Once you have prepared for this question, you would also be ready to answer similar questions such as:

- "What do you know about us?"
- "Tell us something about our organization that isn't common knowledge."
- "How do we differ from our competitors?"
- "If you were in charge of our organization, what would you do differently and why?"
- "What do you see as the strengths and shortcomings of our business?"

"Why should we hire you?"

Use this gift of a question to reiterate your top three or four qualities or skills. Remember that in delivering your response, you have to sound and behave as if you want the job. So focus both on what you say as well as how you say it.

Consider these two examples:

- "From my reading of your job advert, I understand that you are looking for someone who has excellent communication and influencing skills, a high degree of technical expertise and a willingness to go the extra mile for customers. I believe that I meet the brief in all of those aspects. I can talk you through several examples of how I have explained highly technical initiatives to customers in very simple language that focuses on the benefits to them rather than on the detail; in every instance, I work to understand what their particular needs are so that I can meet them in every way. And in terms of willingness to go the extra mile, just the other week, a customer overseas sent me an email and I happened to be online at 2am and responded it to it immediately – and the customer actually emailed back that she hadn't expected a response quite so amazingly quickly!"

- "I've already talked through examples of how I've worked ceaselessly to help my team and department to achieve both their monthly and yearly targets. In addition, I also have an extensive network of contacts across the industry, which allows me to keep at the leading edge in terms of ideas and new initiatives in our field. Finally, I have set myself a goal of having the responsibility for leading a team within the next five years, so you know that I shall be working tirelessly to achieve that."

148

Rookie Buster

Remember that in delivering your response, you have to sound and behave as if you want the job.

"What are your main strengths?"

This question is really just a variation on "Why should we hire you?" However, I have included it to give you further examples of how to emphasize the key reasons why the interviewers should pick you over the other candidates.

Remember that the answer you give to the interviewer at one organization may need to differ from the answer you give to another. Have a look again at the two job adverts for a similar role at ABC Banking Corporation and XYZ Home Trading (on page 44 in Chapter 3). While the two jobs are very similar, each organization emphasizes slightly different skills. And, as a smart candidate, you would emphasize different strengths during different interviews too.

Consider the following examples in crafting answers that are right for you:

- "In my last review, my line manager said that I have three key strengths: my analytical skills, creativity and a willingness to take the initiative. She says that she can always rely on me to break complex problems down into smaller chunks that the rest of the team can get working on. In terms of my creativity, I'm always asked by people from the marketing department to sit in on new product development committees to share my thoughts. And I'm the kind of person who enjoys keeping busy, so I'm always on the lookout for ways to make the team work better."

- "My team tells me that I'm a very good manager to work for. They say that I listen to their views before making decisions and once I've made my decisions I give them a lot of autonomy in how they get on with their work. I've been told several times that I'm also a very strong coach as I take a genuine interest in both the development and welfare of the people around me. I think my leadership style has been really important in helping to grow the confidence and ability of my team – and that's why we managed to meet all of our objectives and even succeeded in driving costs down by an additional 2.4 per cent below the target that had been set for us."

"What are your weaknesses?"

Most interviewers who ask about your strengths will also enquire about your weaknesses. Saying that you have no weaknesses will make you seem incredibly arrogant and not the kind of person that an interviewer will want to hire. Revealing some weaknesses shows that you possess self-awareness and a sense of humility. But be careful not to tell the interviewer what you think your actual faults or flaws may be.

A safer route is to choose a couple of weaknesses that in no way affect your ability to do the job for this organization. For example, if you are applying for a job in data inputting, then you may be able to admit quite safely that you aren't very good at giving presentations. If you're being interviewed for a job as a senior manager, you could admit to being poor at administration and attention to trivial detail.

Rookie Buster

Revealing some weaknesses shows that you possess self-awareness and a sense of humility.

150   When talking about a weakness, you must finish your response by describing how you compensate for or have worked to overcome your weakness. Use these examples to create your own answers:

- "I have to admit that I'm not very good at working on my own. I thrive off the energy of having people around me and having customers or colleagues to work with. So that's why I enjoy working in sales and why I want to work for a dynamic business such as yours where I will constantly be working collaboratively with the rest of the team in the pursuit of new customers."

- "I'm not very good at doing the admin that I know I should be doing. But thankfully I'm in a position now where I can rely on my personal assistant to handle my diary and paperwork for me."

Rookie Buster

When talking about a weakness, you must finish your response by describing how you compensate for or have worked to overcome your weakness.

"Do you have any questions for us?"

Almost all interviewers will give you the opportunity to ask questions. You may be tempted to respond: "No, because you've already answered all of my questions, thank you." But that could be a mistake.

Asking intelligent questions signals intelligence. Questions demonstrate your keenness and interest in the job. And the right questions can reinforce that you really have done your research on the employer.

Rookie Buster

Questions demonstrate your keenness and interest in the job.

Avoiding the wrong questions

But before I tell you how to answer this question, let's consider topics that you definitely must never bring up. In order not to appear greedy or lazy, be sure to avoid asking about:

- The salary, bonuses, benefits or other issues related to your remuneration package.
- The working hours, the need for overtime, or your holiday entitlement.

Of course you may want to know the answers to those questions. Many employers will provide that kind of information on their website or in the recruitment literature (such as their information pack or the original job advert). If an employer does not provide that information, at least wait until *after* you have been offered the job before asking about it.

Another rule in deciding what questions to ask is to ask only for information that you could not have gathered in your research. For example, asking about the organization's new products would be foolish if the organization's website or other literature has pages of information about planned product launches.

152   Asking the right questions

Choose carefully the questions you ask. Consider the following list of
questions that you may ask – but only if you are sure that you should
not already have found the answers out in some other way.

Here are some questions about the day-to-day work:

- "I've read about the job description online, but could you talk me
  through your experience of what the typical working day looks
  like?"
- "What kind of training would I receive to begin with?"
- "Why has this position become available?"
- "What do you see as the key tasks for success in this role?"
- "How would my performance be evaluated?"
- "Looking towards the future, what are the prospects for people
  who start in this role?"

You may also wish to ask about the culture of the organization –
that is, what it's like to be a part of the team:

- "How would you describe the culture around here?"
- "What kinds of people do well within the organization – and why?"
- "When other people have joined and not worked out, what do you
  think they did or didn't do?"
- "Would you mind if I asked why you decided to join the
  organization?"

Tailoring your questions

Remember to tailor your questions based on what you already know
about the organization. You can make the strongest impact by mentioning some piece of insight or information and using it to lead into
a question. Consider these examples:

- "My reading of analyst reports suggests that you're moving out of
  selling directly to consumers and will be focusing more on
  businesses. How would that affect this department?"
- "One of your press releases on the website says that you're

planning to open 35 new stores nationwide. Realistically, what are
the opportunities for someone at my level to get involved in that
expansion over the next 18 months?"

154

Coach's notes

- Always answer questions that invite you to talk about yourself by talking about your recent career and highlighting your most relevant two or three skills.
- Do enough research to ensure you can talk about a handful of reasons you wish to take on this specific role with this particular employer; avoid at all costs talking about why you may wish to leave a bad situation elsewhere.
- Before an interview, list the top handful of your skills that will be of most interest to that particular employer. By doing that, you will be ready to answer any questions about your strengths or why they should hire you.
- Be ready to admit some minor weakness, as saying you have none smacks of arrogance. However, be sure to mention how you compensate for or have worked to overcome your weakness, to reassure employers that your weakness is under control and in no way a concern for them.
- Prepare at least a half-dozen questions to answer during the interview. Saying that you have no questions could be interpreted by an interviewer as lack of interest on your part.

Go for it! Be confident in your ability to wow the interviewers. Avoid trying to memorize answers to the many questions that could crop up. However, do sketch out approximately what you would say to this handful of the most common questions. Honestly, these questions come up time and again, so other job hunters (but not you!) are stupid not to put in the thinking. Prepare the key points you want to get across, and you can ace that interview!

156 Notes

Notes

Putting together a great CV and giving a fantastic interview performance will take you 90 per cent of the way to getting the job offer you
want. In this final chapter, I talk you through the final steps you need
to take once the interviews are over. And, in the unlikely event that
you're not getting the success you want, I take you through trouble-
shooting too.

CHAPTER 10

Closing the deal

Ensuring you have glowing references

Employers usually make job offers subject to "satisfactory" references – in other words, checking that your current or previous employers don't say anything too bad about you. Of course you'd be devastated to be offered a job only to lose it because your references aren't good enough. So make sure you choose your referees (the people who write your references) carefully.

Keeping references off your CV

For a start, don't include details of your references on your CV – it takes up space and you definitely don't want possible future employers to contact your referees until you have been made a firm offer.

You don't even need to include the phrase "References available on request" on your CV: it adds nothing. Employers will ask for references if they want them. In fact, including the phrase may even *detract* from

160   your CV because it is such an obvious statement that you may come across as a bit of a novice or even an idiot!

Choosing the right referee

Amazingly, some job hunters ask former bosses or colleagues to write references for them without checking that those references will help them to get the job. To ensure that you have positive references, always speak to potential referees. Ask them whether they would be happy to give you an unreservedly positive reference.

If a potential referee sounds at all hesitant or reluctant to be totally positive about you, you should politely enquire as to any concerns. Only if you are 100 per cent certain that a referee is willing to speak well of you should you accept them as a referee.

Rookie Buster

To ensure that you have positive references, always speak to potential referees.

Highlighting your strengths to a referee

A great way to ensure that your reference will be consistent with what you have said about yourself in an interview is to write a letter to your referee. Remind each referee of the particular skills, qualities or experience that you would like to have included in your reference.

Consider the following example:

Dear Jeremy,

Thank you for agreeing to write a reference on me. As I mentioned on the telephone, I'm applying for a job as a publishing assistant at a variety of magazine companies.

I'd really appreciate it if you could emphasize certain qualities from when I worked in your team:

- My research skills – for example the work you asked me to do in preparing for your client meetings with Oceanfresh Seafood and Olympus TV Productions.
- My dedication to the team – for example, that I was usually one of the last to leave the office. Remember that time when you told me to go home because you thought I was working too hard! Also that I did not take one sick day and that I was always on time in the mornings too.
- My attention to detail such as when entering our weekly budget data into the spreadsheet for accounts.

I'll give you a call in the next few days to see if you have any questions. Thanks again for agreeing to be a referee in the meantime.

Best regards,
Hilary

Following up with a note

Here's a tip that will boost your chances of getting the job – and it'll take just five minutes. Be sure to write a short thank-you letter to interviewers.

You may consider this an old-fashioned practice. But this is precisely why you should write a letter to interviewers. So few candidates write follow-up letters that you are more likely to make an impact. You will stand out by taking those extra few minutes to show that you really want the job. Given that you've invested hours in researching the job and going along to the interview, doesn't it make sense to spend just another five minutes giving yourself the best chance possible of landing the job?

162   Some pointers on targeting your letter:
- Send either an email or a letter in the post. However, many interviewers may not give you their email addresses – in which case a letter will have to do.
- Keep your letter brief – be sure it is no more than a page in length.
- Send your letter on the same day as you had the interview. Carry some letter paper, envelopes and stamps with you so that you can hand-write your letter and post it on the same day.

Rookie Buster

So few candidates write follow-up letters that you are more likely to make an impact.

In your thank-you note, be sure to express the following points:
- That you enjoyed meeting the interviewers and hearing about the team/department/organization's plans.
- That you now want the job even more than you did before you went into the interview, based on what you heard about the job and the organization.
- That you have the perfect skills and experience for the role. Be sure to mention one of the main benefits that you could bring to the role.

Dealing with disappointment

Even the very best candidates get rejected occasionally. You may be an excellent candidate. But perhaps another candidate was just better on the day, or had more experience or better qualifications. You can't always control the outcome of an interview. However, you *can* control how you respond.

As soon after the interview as possible, be sure to review your

performance during the interview by answering the following 163
questions:

- What went well during the interview? What were you pleased with that you should repeat in future interviews?
- How do you think you used your body language and tone of voice during the interview? What could you do differently in your next interview to communicate your enthusiasm and personality?
- Was your appearance and style of dressing appropriate for the interview? What would you change for future interviews?
- What questions (if any) caused you difficulties or problems? How would you answer them next time?
- Did you do the right amount of research? Or should you do more next time?
- What else could you do to improve your interview performance the next time around?

Review how you did every time and you can ensure that you will learn, grow, get better and ultimately get a great job.

Rookie Buster

Review how you did every time and you can ensure that you will learn, grow, get better and ultimately get a great job.

Trouble-shooting specific situations

The advice in this book will help you to overhaul your job hunting prospects. Occasionally though, job hunters will get stuck with a particular problem. Here's some guidance on three common situations.

164 "I'm getting interviews but not job offers"

Some job hunters go along to interviews but can't seem to convert their interviews into job offers. If that's the case for you, start by checking that you are doing enough basic research on employers before you turn up for the interview (see "Researching employers" in Chapter 2). Are you comfortable that you know enough about the employer to be able to answer questions such as why you want the job or why you want to work for that particular organization?

Another common issue is that you may be focusing a lot of your effort on *what* you say, and not enough on *how* you say it. You can do all the thinking you like on what to say, but you will gain so much more by practising your interview responses out loud.

And the best way to practise out loud is by asking friends to run through mock interviews with you. You could either provide your friends with questions that you've been asked or ask your friends to come up with their own questions. And give them permission after the mock interview to tell you the truth. Exactly what do they think you need to change to improve your interview performance?

Rookie Buster

You can do all the thinking you like on what to say, but you will gain so much more by practising your interview responses out loud.

"I'm not getting invited to interviews"

If you're sending off your CV but not getting any interviews, consider these options:

- **Ask for comments on the effectiveness of your CVs and covering letters.** Ask friends or other people within your network if they know of people who actually interview candidates for a living (perhaps because they frequently hire people, or work in human resources or recruitment). Show those individuals your CV and the covering letters you have used for actual jobs. Ask for their advice. How could you make your applications stronger?

- **Consider applying to different types of organization**. If you don't have quite the right experience or qualifications, you may be better off applying to smaller organizations. Large organizations often have rigid policies about the experience or qualifications they are looking for in candidates. Smaller companies – particularly those with only dozens as opposed to hundreds of employees – are often more flexible with their requirements. Smaller organizations tend to be more interested in finding the right person for the job as opposed to worrying too much about the precise experience or qualifications you may have.

- **Remember the importance of networking**. Look back to Chapter 5 and remind yourself that up to 85 per cent of jobs (that's nearly 9 in every 10) are filled by word of mouth. So ask yourself: are you spending 80 or 90 per cent of your time networking, speaking to acquaintances, gathering information on possible jobs and growing your network of contacts? If you're not, then be sure to invest more of your time in networking rather than simply sending CVs and letters off to prospective employers.

Rookie Buster

Are you spending 80 or 90 per cent of your time networking, speaking to acquaintances, gathering information on possible jobs and growing your network of contacts?

166   "I'm networking, but not getting recommended for jobs"

Many, many job hunters speak about the successes they have had in networking and asking for the support of friends and acquaintances in looking for a new job. The sheer volume of candidates who have found new jobs through networking proves that it works.

But if your networking efforts have yet to pay off, consider the following:

- **Are you managing your personal impact?** Remember that you must stay upbeat and professional in all of your dealings with people when networking. No matter how desperate or despondent you may occasionally feel, you must ensure that the people you meet see you at your best at all times. If you're unsure how you come across when networking, arrange with a friend to run through a mock networking scenario and ask for candid feedback on how you came across.

- **Are you gaining enough referrals?** Remember also that you must take the initiative and ask for the names of further people that you could contact. The purpose of networking is only partly to gather information and advice; a large part of networking is to do with expanding your network. So be certain to ask (politely) for names of other people who could help.

- **Are you putting in enough effort and retaining the initiative?** Bear in mind that people are busy and may forget to return your calls or get in touch with you. You must stay in control – it is *your* responsibility to call people back, write thank-you notes, email them and remind them that you exist!

Rookie Buster

No matter how desperate or despondent you may occasionally feel, you must ensure that the people you meet see you at your best at all times.

Signing on the dotted line

With a little work, you will soon be getting job offers. To ensure that you make a smooth transition into a perfect job, work through the following steps:

1. Wait until you have been made a verbal offer before raising the issue of pay and benefits. The best time to negotiate is when there is no doubt that the employer wants to hire you – but doesn't yet have you. Be polite and calm in all of your negotiations, but remember that if you don't ask, you won't get!

2. Be sure to see the offer in writing. You don't want to quit your old job until your new employer has made a firm offer to you in writing.

3. Evaluate carefully the written offer. Is the salary and benefits package exactly what had been discussed? Are you getting the holiday entitlement that you had expected? Check that you are happy with all of the details before signing on the dotted line.

4. Celebrate! Congratulate yourself on your new job!

Rookie Buster

The best time to negotiate is when there is no doubt that the employer wants to hire you – but doesn't yet have you.

168

Coach's notes

- Be sure to ask potential referees if they would be willing to provide you with wholly positive endorsements; and write them a briefing letter to ensure that they tell employers what you want them to say.
- Follow up every interview by writing a short note to the interviewers. Just five minutes of additional work could make the crucial difference to securing that job!
- Realize that not even the most talented candidates get offered a job every time. To help you improve every time, be sure to quiz yourself to see what you could learn from interview rejections.
- If you are struggling to find a job, remember that networking and using word of mouth referrals is possibly *the* most successful route to finding a new job.
- Bear in mind that the best time to negotiate a better deal is once an employer has made you an offer. Ask (politely) for more and you may just get it!

Go for it! I've been interviewing candidates and training interviewers for years. You now have all of the tools you need to get out there and find yourself a great new job. So what are you waiting for? Go do it. Get a new, better, more fulfilling job. Good luck!

170

Notes

Index

Introduction

Welcome to *Job Hunting for Rookies*. Congratulate yourself as you hold in your hands a tried-and-tested method for getting a job – a job that will both pay you well and allow you to be happy.

If you want practical advice that will help you to find the right job for you, then you're in the right place. Perhaps you are just starting out in your career and looking for your first job, or have been working for quite a few years but want to move on. You could be working full- or part-time at the moment, or maybe you have been out of work for a while. You could be hunting for a job that is exactly the same as what you have always done or looking to make a complete career change. Whatever your situation, I promise to act as your guide and take you step-by-step through the job hunting process.

A book with a difference

Now, I have to admit that there are other books on job hunting. But *Job Hunting for Rookies* is different. Because I'm different. I interview for a living. I train interviewers in how to interview candidates. I help employers to decide what questions they should be asking and the answers they should be listening out for. I've sifted through endless piles of CVs and decided which ones to keep or throw in the bin. I've winced countless times when candidates fall into job hunting traps,

8 but I've also congratulated many candidates when they have aced the interview and gained the job offer of their dreams.

I'm well known for being a careers expert. My advice on careers and job hunting has been featured in top newspapers including the *Daily Telegraph*, the *Guardian* and the *Sunday Times*. And when the BBC decided to broadcast a television series aimed at helping people to find jobs called *How to Get Your Dream Job*, who did they ask to present it? Me, of course.

So trust me when I say that I know how to find the right job for you. Whatever your situation, I can take you from rookie to seasoned professional in ten straightforward steps.

Complete career programme or quick fix

Perhaps you are getting ready to look for a new job and intend to use this book to help in your planning and preparation. If that's the case, then the ten chapters of this book take you through a complete programme that will help you to identify the right job for you, write a compelling CV and covering letter, get invitations to interviews, succeed at interviews, and negotiate a great pay package.

Or, if you've already started looking for a job but have hit a snag, you can skip to the right chapter for you straight away:

- If you're sending out CVs but not getting invited to interviews, go to Chapters 3 and 4. Once you've read those two chapters, work through Chapter 5 as well.
- If you are going to interviews but not receiving offers, head to Chapters 6, 7, 8 and 9.
- If you want to deal with interview nerves and feel more confident, go to Chapter 6.
- If you struggle to come up with good questions to ask during an interview, jump to Chapter 9.
- If you are thinking of changing career, read up on the advice within Chapter 1.
- If your references are letting you down, have a look at Chapter 10.